体育英语专业系列教材

总主编 田 慧

综合英语教程
AN INTEGRATED ENGLISH COURSE

（第二册）

主　编：韩　冰　柳莉蕊
副主编：李　晶　李海英

编　委：王　严　李海英　李　晶
　　　　陈　杰　周春红　柳莉蕊
　　　　赵　雪　袁　哲　韩　冰

审　校：田　慧　Carol Griffiths　Vera Lee

图书在版编目（CIP）数据

综合英语教程.2/ 田慧总主编.—北京：北京大学出版社，2009.3
（体育英语专业系列教材）
ISBN 978-7-301-14494-7

Ⅰ.综… Ⅱ.田… Ⅲ.体育–英语–高等学校–教材 Ⅳ.H31

中国版本图书馆CIP数据核字(2009)第019199号

书　　　名	综合英语教程（第二册）
	ZONGHE YINGYU JIAOCHENG (DI-ER CE)
著作责任者	田　慧　总主编
责 任 编 辑	徐万丽
标 准 书 号	ISBN 978-7-301-14494-7
出 版 发 行	北京大学出版社
地　　　址	北京市海淀区成府路 205 号　100871
网　　　址	http://www.pup.cn
电　　　话	邮购部 010-62752015　发行部 010-62750672　编辑部 010-62759634
电 子 信 箱	zln0120@163.com
印 刷 者	北京虎彩文化传播有限公司
经 销 者	新华书店
	787 毫米 × 1092 毫米　16 开本　14.75 印张　295 千字
	2009 年 3 月第 1 版　2020 年 9 月第 3 次印刷
定　　　价	30.00 元（配有光盘）

未经许可，不得以任何方式复制或抄袭本书之部分或全部内容。
版权所有，侵权必究
举报电话：010-62752024　电子信箱：fd@pup.pku.edu.cn
图书如有印装质量问题，请与出版部联系，电话：010-62756370

前　言

　　从 2002 年开始,国内的体育院校纷纷开设了体育英语专业,培养在体育领域从事对外交流工作的国际体育人才。经过 5 年多发展,体育英语专业既显示出强大的生机和活力,又面临着诸多困难,首要的问题就是教材问题。目前,体育英语专业大多在技能类课程,特别是基础阶段课程中沿用了全国统编英语专业教材。这些教材选材精当、设计合理,对夯实学生语言基本功起到巨大作用,但针对性不强,未能体现出本专业特色。因此,从 2004 年开始,我们就着手策划编写一套供体育英语专业学生使用的系列教材,并于 2007 年获得北京高等教育精品教材立项。系列教材包括基础阶段的《综合英语教程》、《英语听说教程》、《英语阅读教程》和高级阶段的《体育英语阅读》等,首批推出的是基础阶段的《综合英语教程》和《英语听说教程》。

　　经教育部批准的《高等学校英语专业英语教学大纲》指出:英语专业学生应具有扎实的语言基本功、宽广的知识面、一定的相关专业知识、较强的能力和较高素质。基础阶段的教材正是按照这一培养目标编写,立足于加强学生语言基本功,在培养语言基本功的同时渗透体育元素、人文精神,以提高学生的体育知识水平和人文素养,并在设计中力图培养学生的跨文化交际能力和独立思维能力。同时,本系列教材的一个突出特点是将各门课程的同一单元统一于一个话题,学生在综合英语、英语阅读、英语听说中同步围绕一个话题进行不同的技能训练,也使得他们能从不同角度认识同一问题。

　　《综合英语教程》是为第一、二学年的专业基础教学配备的课本,训练听说读写译等各方面技能。教程没有将语法和语言功能作为编写主线,而是以课文的主题和内容作为编写的基础;每一单元围绕同一主题选编了两篇文章,并将有关的体育内容穿插其中。Text I 作为主课文,教师课堂精讲,并处理与课文相关的课文理解、词汇、翻译等练习;Text II 是对本单元话题的扩展和深化,只配课文理解练习和话题讨论,目的在于开拓学生思路,就相关问题提出自己的观点和见解,从而培养学生分析问题和解决问题的能力。课文后设计了综合能力训练和口语活动及写作练习,进一步巩固本单元的知识,加强语言应用能力,同时为参加全国英语专业四级考试做准备。通过每个单元两篇课文的学习和各种练习,学生可对每单元话题的认识加深,在掌握语言知识、加强语言技能的基础上,还能就话题进行口头、笔头交流,陈述观点,发表意见。

本教程课文大都选自英美原文,为了方便教学个别地方我们做了删节和微小的改动。在选材时,我们注重体育专业与人文通识并重,注重内容的专业性和人文性,在英语学习中既学到体育知识,又增加人文知识,提高人文素养。有关体育方面的课文均选自国外的体育教科书,有极强的针对性。

《综合英语教程(第二册)》共 12 个单元,供体育英语专业一年级第二学期教学使用。按照综合英语课程每学期 96 个学时的教学时数,每单元需用 8 个学时完成教学,各校在使用时也可以根据需要进行调整。

编纂过程中,外籍专家 Vera Lee、Carol Griffiths 先后改写了部分课文,在此谨表谢忱。教程选材过程中,参阅了大量英美国家报纸杂志和有关教科书,对一些文章进行了选编,在此谨向原著者致以谢意。

北京体育大学外语系承担了本系列教材的编写工作。由于经验和水平限制,书中不当之处在所难免,敬请使用本教程的师生批评指正。

教程编写完成之际,北京奥运会已成功落下帷幕,中国实现了举办一届"高水平,有特色"的奥运会的目标。欣逢盛世,相信 2008 年奥运会后,我国的体育事业必将迎来一个崭新的发展机遇期,对外交流也会日益扩大。随着全球化的不断深入,国际体育交往愈发凸显其重要性,中国亟须引进国外先进的体育科学理论、训练方法、休闲理念和健康的生活方式。我们期待,本套教程能对提高我国体育英语专业的建设水平,培养更多的国际体育人才,进而提高我国的体育发展水平贡献绵薄之力。

编者

2008 年 12 月

TABLE OF CONTENTS

Unit 1 Family ·· **1**
    Text I   Kinship and the Family / 1
    Text II   A Father's Walk to School / 10

Unit 2 Jobs ·· **17**
    Text I   Why People Work / 17
    Text II   Making the Best of a Good Job / 28

Unit 3 Business ··· **35**
    Text I   Japanese Style in Decision-Making / 35
    Text II   Playing to Win / 47

Unit 4 Music ·· **54**
    Text I   Music and Healing / 54
    Text II   Sport and Music / 66

Unit 5 Disasters ··· **74**
    Text I   We Are the Problem / 75
    Text II   After the Tornado / 85

Unit 6 Legends and Myths ·· **92**
    Text I   Modern Mythology / 92
    Text II   Prometheus Steals Fire—A Myth of Ancient Greeks / 103

Unit 7 Shopping ··· **109**
    Text I   A Pair of Silk Stockings (I) / 110
    Text II   A Pair of Silk Stockings (II) / 121

Unit 8   Women around the World ··· **128**
    Text I   The Feminine Mystique / 128
    Text II Still a Perfect 10 / 138

Unit 9   Travel ··· **146**
    Text I   Transformative Travel / 146
    Text II Sport and Tourism to Stimulate Development / 158

Unit 10 Famous People ··· **166**
    Text I   Jefferson Today / 166
    Text II Kings of Athletes / 179

Unit 11 Health ··· **187**
    Text I   Models of Health / 187
    Text II In Sickness, in Health / 198

Unit 12 Memories ·· **206**
    Text I   The 1896 Olympic Games in Athens / 206
    Text II I Remember... / 219

References ·· **227**

Unit 1 Family

Warm-up Activities

1. A healthy family is a place for comfort, development and regeneration; a place from which we go forth renewed and charged with power for positive living. What are the keys to a strong family? Discuss with your classmates and report to the class.
2. Do you live in an extended family or a nuclear family? Which type of family do you think is more beneficial for people of different ages? Use specific reasons to support your views.

Text I

Kinship and the Family

Pre-reading Questions

1. What changes has the Chinese family structure undergone?
2. How do people in your hometown establish a marriage?

1   Most social anthropologists recognize the family as a basic social unit. In its most elementary form it may be defined as a group consisting of a man and a woman and their children living together in one home. Such a domestic group is known as a nuclear family. It is usually established by means of a formal contract of marriage, but a contract of this kind is not a necessary condition for a nuclear family to exist. It can also exist when a couple and their offspring share a common residence, whether the couple is married or not. In other words, a family may exist even when the relationship between the man and the woman is

one of concubinage rather than one of marriage.

2 Although we can, in general, define the nuclear family as a couple and their children living within the same residential boundary, we must recognize that such a definition is in fact a generalization which may not hold true in particular instances. Sometimes a nuclear family is incomplete

in that one spouse is absent from the household. When a family is incomplete it is usually the man rather than the woman who is away from home. Such a situation may be the result of social convention. For example, among the Ashanti, a tribe in Ghana, spouses continue to reside with their own kin after marriage and do not live together as husband and wife. On the other hand, a nuclear family may be incomplete by reason of economic necessity. Sometimes, for example, a man has to leave his family to work in another part of the country or in a different country altogether. This is the case with many workers in South Africa and with foreign workers in France and Germany.

3 The nuclear family may be extended by the addition of other people living within the same residential boundary. So far we have been assuming that the family is based on a monogamous marriage that it has only one man and one woman living together as husband and wife. But monogamy is only one form of marriage. In societies where polygamy is practised the family will include more than two spouses. In the case of polygyny, it will include one husband and more than one wife; in the case of polyandry, it will include one wife and more than one husband.

4 In both monogamous and polygamous societies, families may also be extended by the addition of related or non-related people. In some, for example, people like servants and workmen live with the family as members of the household. Again, one often finds that families are extended by the addition of consanguineal relatives, or kin, with one or more of the marriage partners, brothers, sisters, fathers, grandfathers and so on. Affinal relatives like brothers-in-law, sisters-in-law and so on may also become members of the family and share a common residence with the brother or sister of their spouses.

5 Relatives, however, are not defined in terms of common residence. The

family exists beyond the limits of the residential boundary and, in many societies, ties of kinship and affinity are recognized by people who in Western Europe would not be regarded as relatives at all. Thus, for example, some societies have terms which refer to one's mother's brother's wife's father (MoBrWiFa), one's father's mother's sister's son's wife (FaMoSiSoWi) and so on. Furthermore, in many societies distinctions are made between relatives which in English-speaking societies are grouped together under the same term. For example, in English we have only one term "grandfather" to refer to FaFa and MoFa, but we often find that these relatives are clearly distinguished by different terms in other languages. The extent to which ties of kinship and affinity are recognized varies widely in different societies. The description of such ties by reference to the terms which are used to talk about them is one of the complex tasks that a social anthropologist has to undertake.

6   We have spoken of marriage as a formal contract. It should be noted, however, that this contract does not take the same form in different societies. In Western societies, the union of a man and a woman is given the status of legal marriage by being registered by an official recognized by the state. In some African societies, however, marriage has nothing to do with an official registration of this kind but is legalized by the formal exchange of goods. Generally it is the bridegroom who is required to make a payment of goods to the bride's kin, though sometimes a payment is also made by the bridegroom's kin to that of the bride.

7   Among the Nuer, a people living in Southern Sudan, the payment made to the bride's kin, known as bridewealth, is in the form of cattle. Once the amount of bridewealth is agreed upon and the formal payment is made, the marriage becomes a legal union and the offspring of the union becomes the legitimate children of the husband. They remain his children even if the wife subsequently leaves him to live with another man. Furthermore, the giving and receiving of bridewealth represents so binding a contract that even if the wife has children by the man with whom she lives with after leaving her husband, these children will legally be her husband's, so long as the cattle offered at the time of marriage remain the property of the wife's kin. The male offspring from the second and illegal union of the woman will inherit not from his real father but from the woman's husband, and the bridewealth given for the female offspring of this second union at the time of their marriage will go not to their real father but to

their mother's legal husband. Thus a distinction has to be made between a natural father, or genitor, and a legal father, or pater, and between natural and legal children.

8   Once a marriage has been made legal by the giving and receiving of bridewealth, it remains a permanent union and cannot be dissolved. Even the death of the husband does not cause dissolution of the marriage. Among the Nuer, a man's heir is his older brother who not only inherits his possessions, but also takes on the domestic responsibilities of his dead brother. This means he becomes the guardian of his brother's widow, or widows, and of his children. If a widow is still young he may live with her as a substitute for her husband, but the children that are born from this union will not be his but his dead brother's. Only when bridewealth is returned can a marriage be dissolved.

9   Though the family is recognized as a basic social unit, its definition is by no means basic when it comes to different cultures' views on marriage, children, and relatives. No matter what kind of family structure people live in, the family unit is where one finds his/her roots and a place where they belong to.

(1,167 words)

Words and Expressions

kinship	/ˈkɪnʃɪp/	n.	a family relationship 亲属关系
anthropologist	/ˌænθrəˈpɒlədʒɪst/	n.	a social scientist who specializes in anthropology 人类学家
elementary	/ˌelɪˈmentərɪ/	adj.	basic or simple 基础的，简单的
nuclear family		n.	a family unit that consists only of a husband, wife and children（仅由夫妻与子女组成的）核心家庭，小家庭
establish	/ɪsˈtæblɪʃ/	vt.	to begin a relationship with someone or a situation that will continue（与某人或某种情况）建立（关系）
contract	/ˈkɒntrækt/	n.	an official agreement between two or more people, stating what each will do 契约，合同
offspring	/ˈɒfsprɪŋ/	n.	someone's child or children（某人的）后代，子女，子孙
residence	/ˈrezɪdəns/	n.	a house, especially a large or official one 住宅 (**residential** adj. 住宅的)

concubinage	/kɔn'kju:bɪndʒ/	n.	cohabitation without being legally married 非法同居
generalization	/ˌdʒenərəlaɪ'zeɪʃən/	n.	a statement about all the members of a group that may be true in some or many situations but is not true in every case 概括,归纳
spouse	/spaʊz/	n.	a husband or wife 配偶
household	/'haʊshəʊld/	n.	all the people who live together in one house 一家人
convention	/kən'venʃən/	n.	behaviour and attitudes that most people in a society consider to be normal and right 习俗,常规
tribe	/traɪb/	n.	a social group consisting of people of the same race who have the same beliefs, customs, language, etc., and usually live in one particular area ruled by their leader 部落,部落社会
reside	/rɪ'zaɪd/	vi.	to live in a particular place 居住
kin	/kɪn/	n.	family and relatives 家人,家属,亲属
necessity	/nɪ'sesɪti/	n.	something that is necessary 必要,需要
extend	/ɪks'tend/	vi./vt.	to (cause something to) reach, stretch or continue; to add to something in order to make it bigger or longer 扩大,延长
monogamy	/mɒ'nɒgəmɪ/	n.	the custom of being married to only one husband or wife 一夫一妻制 **monogamous** adj. 一夫一妻制的
polygamy	/pə'lɪgəmɪ/	n.	the practice of having more than one husband or wife at the same time 多配偶(制)
polygyny	/pɒ'lɪdʒɪnɪ/	n.	having more than one wife at a time 一夫多妻(制) **polygynous** adj. 一夫多妻(制)的
polyandry	/'pɒlɪændrɪ/	n.	having more than one husband at a time 一妻多夫(制) **polyandrous** adj. 一妻多夫(制)的
consanguineal	/ˌkɒnsæŋ'gwɪnɪəl/	adj.	of the same blood 同宗的,血缘的,血亲的
affinity	/ə'fɪnɪtɪ/	n.	kinship by marriage 姻亲关系 **affinal** adj. 姻亲的
vary	/'veərɪ/	vi.	to become different in some particular way, without permanently losing one's or its former characteristics or essence 呈现不同

registration	/ˌredʒɪsˈtreɪʃən/	n.	the act of recording names and details on an official list 登记
legalize	/ˈliːɡəlaɪz/	vt.	to make something legal so that people are allowed to do it 使合法化，使得到法律认可
bridewealth	/ˈbraɪdwelθ/	n.	an amount of money or property or wealth paid by the groom or his family to the parents of a woman upon the marriage of their daughter to the groom 聘礼
legitimate child(ren)			合法婚姻所生的子女，婚生的子女
subsequently	/ˈsʌbsɪkwəntlɪ/	adv.	after an event in the past 后来，随后
binding	/ˈbaɪndɪŋ/	adj.	executed with proper legal authority 具有法律约束力的
legally	/ˈliːɡəlɪ/	adv.	according to the law 法律上，依据法律
inherit	/ɪnˈherɪt/	vi./vt.	to receive money, property, etc. from someone after they have died 继承(遗产)
genitor	/ˈdʒenɪtə/	n.	a natural father 生父
pater	/ˈpeɪtə/	n.	father 父亲
dissolve	/dɪˈzɒlv/	vt.	to formally end a marriage 解除婚姻关系
dissolution	/ˌdɪsəˈluːʃən/	n.	the act of formally ending a marriage 正式解除婚姻关系
heir	/eə/	n.	the person who has the legal right to receive the property or title of another person when they die (财产等的)继承人
guardian	/ˈɡɑːdjən/	n.	someone who is legally responsible for someone else, especially a child (尤指儿童的)监护人

Reading Comprehension

I. Define the following terms with the information from the text.

1. polygyny:

2. polygamy:

3. polyandry:

Unit 1   Family

II. **Summarize the following situations according to the text.**
　　1. Western societies vs some African societies in respect of marriage: _____
　　_____
　　_____

　　2. After the death of the husband in a Nuer family: _____
　　_____
　　_____

III. **Answer the following questions.**
　　1. What is the definition of a nuclear family?
　　2. What might be the reason for the incompleteness of a nuclear family?
　　3. How can a nuclear family be extended?
　　4. What is your understanding of families formed by concubinage rather than marriage?
　　5. What are some difficulties in using the English word *father* in describing the Nuer family?

IV. **Judge, according to the text, whether the following statements are true or false. For false statements, write the facts in parentheses.**
　　1. A contract of marriage is a necessity for a nuclear family to exist.
　　　(　　　　　　　　　　　　　　　　　　　　　　　　　　　　　)
　　2. The man's absence from the household is caused by economic reasons.
　　　(　　　　　　　　　　　　　　　　　　　　　　　　　　　　　)
　　3. In the case of polygyny, it includes more than two spouses.
　　　(　　　　　　　　　　　　　　　　　　　　　　　　　　　　　)
　　4. In some African societies, marriage is legalized by the formal exchange of goods.
　　　(　　　　　　　　　　　　　　　　　　　　　　　　　　　　　)
　　5. Among the Nuer, the bridewealth of a female offspring goes to the biological father.
　　　(　　　　　　　　　　　　　　　　　　　　　　　　　　　　　)
　　6. A relative in the Chinese culture is not necessarily considered a relative in the European culture.
　　　(　　　　　　　　　　　　　　　　　　　　　　　　　　　　　)

Vocabulary Exercises

I. **Fill in each blank with one of the following words from each pair and note the difference in meaning between them. Change the form when necessary.**

   1. CONTRACT   CONTACT
      a. The actor has signed a seven-year _____ with a Hollywood studio.
      b. Have you been in _____ with Andy recently?
      c. The firm could take legal action against you if you break the _____.
      d. He lost _____ with old school friends after graduation.

   2. BOUNDARY   BORDER
      a. The Mississippi River forms a natural _____ between Iowa and Illinois.
      b. We crossed the Mexican _____ into the USA in the dark.
      c. The two governments have settled their differences over their common _____.
      d. The blurring of the _____ between high and low culture is one of the main complaints made by traditional intellectuals about contemporary mass society.

II. **Fill in the blank in each sentence with a word or phrase taken from the box in its appropriate form.**

residence	by means of	polygamous	dissolve
undertake	affinity	speak of	agree (up)on
inherit	permanent		

   1. It was the first time she had ever _____ marriage.
   2. Jeff now _____ in southern France, but he is still a US citizen.
   3. She seems to have a natural _____ with animals.
   4. Thanks to the efforts of the UN Secretary-General, the two sides _____ a cease-fire.
   5. The disease can cause _____ damage to your brain.
   6. In California, _____ of marriage can be granted if the court finds there are "irreconcilable differences" between husband and wife.

7. _____ is rare in modern society, but was quite common in ancient times.
8. The large _____ from his uncle meant that he could buy whatever he wanted.
9. Alexander and his team _____ the task of compiling a comprehensive English dictionary in the 1970s.
10. The deaf girl tried to explain _____ sign language.

III. Choose a word that best completes each of the following sentences.

1. She was _____ as a laboratory assistant in the university.
   A. taken on   B. taken in   C. taken over   D. taken away
2. Your story doesn't agree _____ what the witnesses have told us.
   A. on   B. with   C. to   D. about
3. _____ money, I was better off in my last job.
   A. By means of   B. In line with   C. With regard to   D. In terms of
4. I don't usually side with the management, but in this _____ I agree with what they're saying.
   A. incidence   B. insurance   C. instance   D. instant
5. Many personnel managers say it is getting harder and harder to _____ honest applicants from the growing number of dishonest ones.
   A. dissolve   B. distinguish   C. discount   D. disguise

Translation Exercises

Translate each of the following sentences into English, using the word or phrase given in the brackets.

1. 爱因斯坦发现了很多令人惊叹的定理，这些定理至今仍然适用。(hold true)

2. 电视提供了来自世界各地的信息，扩展了孩子的视野；但另一方面，电视也会使孩子变得被动和懒惰。(on the other hand)

3. 迄今为止，我从未听说我们学校有学生因学费昂贵而辍学。(so far)

4. 那对双胞胎姐妹不仅长相惊人地相似,而且行为举止、兴趣爱好也相同,人们很难把她们区分开来。(distinguish)

5. 两国代表团未能在降低关税的问题上达成一致,谈判不欢而散。(agree upon)

6. 只要我们齐心协力,就一定能渡过难关,战胜这场重大的自然灾害。(so long as)

7. 做完手术后,医生警告他不要再承担繁重的工作,否则,后果不堪设想。(take on)

8. 虽然电脑在我们日常生活和工作中发挥了极其重要的作用,但是它永远不会成为人脑的替代品。(substitute)

Text II

A Father's Walk to School

Pre-reading Questions

1. Did your parents often accompany you to elementary school? How did you feel about your parents' companionship?
2. Did your parents spend a lot of time with you when you were a kid? Do you think it was beneficial to your development?

1   I stand by the front door watching the neighborhood kids materialize out of thin air like droplets of dew, scores of them, racing toward school. One minute the street is empty, the next it's awash in color as children hurtle around corners, leap over hedges, and emerge from minivans dressed in reds, greens, yellows, and blues. Their book bags jangle, their sneakers are half laced, and traces of milk whiten their upper lips. They run singly and in mobs, waving to departing parents, the crossing guard, and the janitor. It's 8:30 a.m., and the

school day is about to begin.

2 When we moved to this neighborhood in Scarsdale, N.Y., 16 years ago, few things gave me more pleasure than walking the kids to school. I was one of a few fathers who got to enjoy that daily ritual. Most of my neighbors were on the train or behind their desks by 8:30—many of them relieved they didn't have to wrestle their kids into coats, wipe their  faces, brush their hair, make sure that last week's library book was in the backpack along with that day's homework and lunch. But not only was that my favorite time of day, it was my favorite destination.

3 As much as I loved the morning walk—holding fast to my children's hands as they balanced along the curbstones—it was the kindergarten classroom itself that drew me from the house, its enchantments as palpable to me as they were to my kids. There, the young students were greeted by a 15-pound, floppy-eared rabbit, two canaries, a bucket of tadpoles, a tropical fish tank, and a teacher as benevolent as the atmosphere she inhabited. Against one wall was a cozy fireplace, a rocking chair, and a well-stocked bookcase. Another area offered crayons and paints for budding artists; incipient architects and engineers could play with blocks; young botanists could observe the peas and beans which sprouted from Dixie cups.

4 It was hard to head home from such a fertile world—the sunlight streaming through tall windows, the chatter of curious children filling the air. In every corner something profound was being discovered. I wanted to sit on the floor and encounter life from that perspective, live as though the next minute would unlock secrets as transforming as the rules of reading. I wanted to return home exhilarated by the acquisition of new skills, new thoughts, and new feelings.

5 But finally the late bell would ring, and the teacher would call her students together. Parents tendered last-minute instructions, adjusted misbuttoned shirts, and melted away. But on some mornings, I would linger to watch the children's faces illumine with curiosity and perception as they discussed the weather and the world.

6 Reluctantly, I would tear myself from that room and return home to begin my own work. The neighborhood stood colorless and quiet. Behind me the brick

schoolhouse teemed with the energy of 300 young minds. Periodically, as if to vent some of that energy, it released small clouds of children onto the playground for half an hour of supervised chaos. At my desk a block away, I paused to listen to the shouting and singing. The mingled voices reminded me of my own early days of wonder.

7   What is it about those years of elementary school that seemed so enviable in retrospect? Perhaps it's the seamlessness of a child's being and ambition. Set free on the playground, they launch themselves into small fulfillments. Very young children rarely speak of frustrated hopes and unfulfilled desires. They know only one way to be: boisterously or softly expressive of their basic nature: genuine. And they live wholly in the present, absorbed in the task at hand, convinced of its absolute rightness and necessity. From an adult vantage of gnawing doubt, constant reevaluation, and a hyperawareness of time, it seems a singularly blessed state.

8   At 3 p.m., the morning tide would reverse as all those noisy, colorful kids burst through the school's double doors and spilled across the sidewalk like flood waters seeking lower ground. Outside the kindergarten classrooms, I would watch the "upperclassmen" emerge. The fourth—and fifth-grade boys would shout, shove, and run. The girls would group together protectively, often holding hands. The older kids were an altogether different species from the little ones, still appearing so defenseless.

9   A moment later, the youngest students would appear, struggling to push open the wooden doors, their eyes searching for their guardians. I would think, awaiting the appearance of my firstborn: "She isn't that small, is she?" At home she was our "big girl," towering over her toddler brother and sister. But beside the rowdy "upperclassmen" she seemed heartbreakingly vulnerable. After seeing me, she would race into my arms. I would realize anew how small she still was, and why I loved this ritual of separation and return. It wasn't simply the inviting riches of the classroom but the yielding up of my most precious possession and the cheerful anticipation of her homecoming each afternoon. I thrilled for that moment of reunion, that brief explosion of relief and gratitude that animated her searching eyes, and the grasp of her leaping arms.

10 And then almost as soon as that cordon of comfort had been established, she would break free, hand me her backpack and a crumpled announcement from her teacher, and ask if her friend Benedicte could come home to play.

Unit 1   Family

After a brief negotiation with Benedicte's mother, the two girls would clasp hands and skip away, the remainder of the afternoon stretching before them in a sweet haze of snacks and games and 5-year-old communion. I would hurry after them, borne along by the colorful tide of children, a whale among minnows, grateful for the gift of such exuberant company.

(957 words)

Reading Comprehension

I. **Answer the following questions with the information you read from the passage.**
   1. What can you learn from the description of children at the beginning of the school day?
   2. Why did the kindergarten attract the father from the house?
   3. Why did the father say the years of elementary school seemed so enviable in retrospect?
   4. What made the father realize he was the guardian of his "big girl" while waiting for her at the school gate?

II. **Topics for discussion and reflection.**
   1. Will children lose their independence if parents often walk them to school?
   2. What difference would it have made if your parents had given you more/less attention when you were young?

Exercises for Integrated Skills

I. **Dictation**

   Listen to the following passage. Altogether the passage will be read to you four times. During the first reading, which will be read at normal speed, listen and try to understand the meaning. For the second and third readings, the passage will be read sentence by sentence, or phrase by phrase, with intervals of 15 to 20 seconds. The last reading will be done at normal speed again and during this time you should check your work. You will then be given 2 minutes to check through your work once more.

II. Cloze

Fill in each blank in the passage below with a word or phrase taken from the box in its appropriate form.

spontaneous	checkout	physical	recede	surprise
exuberant	exchange	playful	honest	treasure
run through	parent	all-out	look	cover
understand	roll-up	nonstop	thrill	blast

I have a friend who is falling in love. She ___1___ claims the sky is bluer. Mozart moves her to tears. She has lost 15 pounds and looks like a ___2___ girl.

"I'm young again!" she shouts ___3___.

As my friend raves about her new love, I've taken a good ___4___ at my old one. My husband of almost 20 years, Scott, has gained 15 pounds. Once a marathon runner, he now runs only down hospital halls. His hairline is ___5___ and his body shows the signs of long working hours and too many candy bars. Yet he can still give me a certain look across a restaurant table and I want to ask for the check and head home.

When my friend asked me "What will make this love last?" I ___6___ all the obvious reasons: commitment, shared interests, unselfishness, ___7___ attraction, and communication. Yet there's more. We still have fun. ___8___ good times. Yesterday, after slipping the rubber band off the ___9___ newspaper, Scott flipped it ___10___ at me: this led to an ___11___ war. Last Saturday at the grocery store, we split the list and raced each other to see who could make it to the ___12___ first. Even washing dishes can be a ___13___. We enjoy simply being together.

And there are ___14___ . One time I came home to find a note on the front door that led me to another note, then another, until I reached the walk-in closet. I opened the door to find Scott holding a "pot of gold" (my cooking kettle) and the "___15___" of a gift package. Sometimes I leave him notes on the mirror and little presents under his pillow.

There is ___16___ . I understand why he must play basketball with the guys. And he understands why, once a year, I must get away from the house, the kids—and even him—to meet my sisters for a few days of ___17___ talking and laughing.

There is sharing. Not only do we share household worries and ___18___ burdens—we also share ideas. Scott came home from a convention last month and presented me with a thick historical novel. Though he prefers ___19___ and science fiction, he had read the novel on the plane. He touched my heart when he explained it was because he wanted to be able to ___20___ ideas about the book after I'd read it.

Oral Activities

Activity One: Story telling of parental love.

Tell a story about parental love in class, and state some of your viewpoints on how to treat child(ren) properly.

Activity Two: Work in groups and discuss the following questions.

1. Do your parents have a strong influence on you? If so, in what ways?
2. What are the differences between a father's love and a mother's love?
3. What are the factors that can make one's family stable?

Activity Three: Family Violence

"Family Violence" is a term that includes many different forms of abuse, mistreatment or neglect that adults or children may experience in their intimate, kinship or dependent relationships. According to a survey reported by the *China Consumer Journal* in 2003, family violence occurred in about 30 percent of China's 270 million households with about 90 percent of the abusers being male.

1. From your perspective, what might be the reasons that cause family violence? How can the problem be solved?
2. In groups, stage a short play, or a talk show, with one person as an expert on family issues, counseling a woman or a child who suffers from family violence.

Writing Practice

Note Writing: A Note of Explanation

Your parents are out shopping and you receive a call from a friend inviting you to visit him/her in another district of the city. You may not return home for dinner. Write a message to your parents to explain this.

_____ February, 20 _____

Dear Mom and Dad,

Love,

Composition Writing

Write a composition about how your parents show their love for you in about 120 words. Detailed examples should be included in the composition.

Unit 2 Jobs

Warm-up Activities

1. What are your dream jobs? Why are you expecting to take up the jobs?
2. List as many types of jobs as you can think of. Then, in pairs, one describes the job, the other guesses the name of it.

Text I

Why People Work

Pre-reading Questions

1. Do you see work as a burden or an opportunity?
2. In the Chinese society, what is the NUMBER ONE reason for working? What are some of the rewards that people might get from work?

1   Jobs and work do much more than most of us realize to provide happiness and contentment. We're all used to thinking that work provides the material things of life—the goods and services that make possible our modern civilization. But we are much less conscious of the extent to which work provides the more intangible, but more crucial, psychological well-being that can make the difference between a full and an empty life.

2   Historically, work has been associated with slavery and sin, compulsion and punishment. And in our own day we are used to hearing the traditional complaints, "I can't wait for my vacation." "I wish I could stay home today." "My boss treats me poorly." "I've got too much work to do and not enough

time to do it." Against this background, it may well come as a surprise to learn that not only psychologists but other behavioral scientists have come to accept the positive contribution of work to the individual's happiness and sense of per-

sonal achievement. Work is more than a necessity for most human beings; it is the focus of their lives, the source of their identity and creativity.

3   Rather than a punishment or a burden, work is the opportunity to realize one's potential. Many psychiatrists heading mental health clinics have observed its therapeutic effect. A good many patients who languish in clinics, depressed or obsessed, gain renewed self-confidence when gainfully employed, and lose some, if not all, of their most acute symptoms. Increasingly, institutions dealing with mental health problems are establishing workshops wherein those too sick to get a job in "outside" world can work.

4   And the reverse is true, too. For large numbers of people, the absence of work is debilitating. Retirement often brings many problems surrounding the "What do I do with myself?" question, even though there may be no financial cares. Large numbers of people regularly get headaches and other psychosomatic illnesses on weekends when they don't have their jobs to go to, and must fend for themselves. It has been observed that unemployment, quite aside from exerting financial pressures, brings enormous psychological malaise and that many individuals deteriorate rapidly when jobless.

5   But why? Why should work be such a significant source of human satisfaction? A good share of the answer rests in the kind of pride that is stimulated by the job, by the activity of accomplishing.

6   Human beings crave a sense of being accomplished, of being able to do things, with their hands, with their minds, with their wills. We all want to feel we have the ability to do something that is meaningful and that stands outside of ourselves as a tribute to our inherent abilities.

7   It is easiest to see this in the craftsman who lovingly shapes some base material into an object that may be either useful or beautiful or both. You can see the carpenter or bricklayer stand aside and admire the product of his personal skill.

8   But even where there is no obvious end product that is solely attributable to one person's skill, researchers have found that employees find pride in accomplishment. Even the housekeeping and laundry workers take pride in the fact that in their own ways they are helping to cure sick people—and thus accomplishing a good deal.

9   We are often misled by the gripes and complaints surrounding difficult work; deep down most people regard their own capacity to conquer a tough job as a mark of their own unique personality. Grousing is just part of working. After all, how else do you know who you are, except as you can demonstrate the ability of your mind to control your limbs and hands and words? You are, in significant measure, what you can do.

10   Some are deceived into thinking that people like to store up energy, to rest and save themselves as much as possible. Just the opposite. It is energy expenditure that is satisfying.

11   Just watch an employee who must deal with countless other people because his or her job is at some central point in a communication network: a salesman at a busy counter, a stock broker on the phone, a customer representative. They will tell you how much skill and experience it takes to field countless questions and handle a welter of diverse personalities every hour of the day. Not everyone can interact with such persistence and over long hours, but those who do, pride themselves on a distinctive ability that contributes mightily to the running of the organization.

12   But work is more than accomplishment and pride in being able to command the job, because, except for a few artisans and artists, most work takes place "out in the world," with and through other people.

13   Perhaps an example of "Esprit de corps" will make the point:

14   I remember viewing a half dozen men in a chair factory whose job was to bend several pieces of steel and attach them so that a bridge chair would result. While there were ten or twelve of these "teams" that worked together, one in particular was known for its perfect coordination and lightning-like efforts. The men knew they were good. They would work in spurts for twenty or thirty minutes before taking a break—to show themselves, bystanders and other groups, what it was to be superbly skilled and self-controlled, to be the best in the factory.

15   When I talked with them, each expressed enormous pride in being a part of the fastest, best team. And this sense of belonging to an accomplished work group is one of the distinctive satisfactions of the world of work.

16   One further word about work group satisfaction. Unlike many other aspects of life, relationships among people at work tend to be simpler, less complicated, somewhat less emotional. This is not to say there aren't arguments and jealousies, but, on the whole, behavioral research discloses that human relations at work are just easier, perhaps because they are more regular and predictable and thus simpler to adjust to than the sporadic, the more intense and less regular relationships in the community. And the work group also gently pressures its members to learn how to adjust to one another so that the "rough edges" are worked off because people know they must do certain things with and through one another each day.

17   Beyond the team and the work group, there is the organization, whether it be company or hospital or university. The same pride in being part of a well-coordinated, successful unit is derived from being part of a larger collectivity. Working for a company that is thought of as being one of the best in the community can provide employees with both status and self-confidence. They assume, usually with good reason, that others regard them more highly, even envy them, and that they are more competent than the average because of this association with a "winner," a prestigious institution. We in truth bask in the reflected glory of the institution, and we seek ways of asserting our membership so that others will know and can recognize our good fortune.

(1,184 words)

Words and Expressions

contentment	/kən'tentmənt/	n.	the state of being happy and satisfied 满意, 满足
intangible	/ɪn'tændʒəbl/	adj.	that cannot be clearly felt or described 无法形容的, 难以捉摸的
psychological	/ˌsaɪkə'lɒdʒɪkəl/	adj.	of or affecting the mind 精神上的, 心理的
sin	/sɪn/	n.	the offence of breaking, or the breaking of, a religious or moral law 罪, 罪孽

Unit 2　Jobs

compulsion	/kəmˈpʌlʃən/	n.	the act of forcing or influencing someone to do something they do not want to do 强制，强迫
necessity	/nɪˈsesɪtɪ/	n.	something that you need to have in order to live 必需品
potential	/pəˈtenʃəl/	n.	the ability to develop, achieve or succeed 潜力，潜能
therapeutic	/ˌθerəˈpjuːtɪk/	adj.	relating to the treatment or cure of an illness 治病的
languish	/ˈlæŋɡwɪʃ/	vi.	to remain in an unpleasant or unwanted situation, often for a long time 受苦，受煎熬
depressed	/dɪˈprest/	adj.	feeling very unhappy 沮丧的，忧愁的
obsessed	/əbˈsest/	adj.	considering somebody or something as so important that you are always thinking or worrying about them 着迷的，困扰的
renewed	/rɪˈnjuːd/	adj.	starting again 重新产生的
wherein	/weərˈɪn/	adv./conj.	in which place or part 在哪里，在哪方面
reverse	/rɪˈvɜːs/	n.	the exact opposite of what has just been mentioned 正相反
debilitate	/dɪˈbɪlɪteɪt/	vt.	making your body or mind weak 使(身体或精神)虚弱的
psychosomatic	/ˌsaɪkəʊsəˈmætɪk/	adj.	caused by fear or anxiety rather than by a physical problem 由焦虑引起的
aside from			besides 除……以外(包括在内)
exert	/ɪɡˈzɜːt/	vt.	to use a quality, skill, pressure, etc. 用(某特质、技巧、压力等)
malaise	/mæˈleɪz/	n.	general feeling of illness, without clear signs of a particular disease 不适，微恙
deteriorate	/dɪˈtɪərɪəreɪt/	vi.	to become worse 恶化
a tribute to			a clear sign of the good qualities that someone or something has 是(某些优良品质的)标示，证明
inherent	/ɪnˈhɪərənt/	adj.	existing as a natural or basic part of something 固有的，内在的
bricklayer	/ˈbrɪkleɪə/	n.	someone whose job is to build walls, buildings, etc. with bricks 砖瓦匠
solely	/ˈsəʊlɪ/	adv.	only 仅仅

attributable	/əˈtrɪbjutəbəl/	adj.	likely to have been caused by something 可归因于……的
housekeeping	/ˈhaʊskiːpɪŋ/	n.	the work and organization of things that need to be done in a house 料理家务
mislead	/mɪsˈliːd/	vi.	to cause someone to believe something that is not true 误导
gripe	/graɪp/	n.	complaint; expression of discontent 牢骚, 怨言
deep down			secretly know or feel without admitting it 心底, 内心
capacity	/kəˈpæsɪtɪ/	n.	the ability to do something 能力
conquer	/ˈkɒŋkə/	vt.	to gain control over something that is difficult, using a lot of effort 克服, 制服
grouse	/graʊs/	vi.	to complain about something 抱怨, 发牢骚
demonstrate	/ˈdemənstreɪt/	vt.	to show that a person or thing has a particular skill, quality, or ability 展现, 表现出
deceive	/dɪˈsiːv/	vi./vt.	to persuade someone that something false is the truth 欺骗
store up			to put things away and keep them until you need them 储藏, 储存
expenditure	/ɪksˈpendɪtʃə/	n.	the action of spending or using time, money, energy, etc. 耗费, 花费
field	/fiːld/	vt.	to answer questions, telephone calls, etc. successfully, especially when there are a lot of them or the questions are difficult 顺利处理 (一系列问题)
welter	/ˈweltə/	n.	a confused mass, multitude 混乱
diverse	/daɪˈvɜːs/	adj.	very different from each other 各种各样的
interact	/ˌɪntərˈækt/	vi.	to affect each other 相互作用, 相互影响
persistence	/pəˈsɪstəns/	n.	determination to do something even though it is difficult or other people oppose it 坚持不懈
distinctive	/dɪˈstɪŋktɪv/	adj.	having a special quality, character, or appearance that is different and easy to recognize 特别的
mightily	/ˈmaɪtɪlɪ/	adv.	greatly, a lot 非常地, 极大地
running	/ˈrʌnɪŋ/	n.	the process of managing or organizing a business, home, organization, etc. 经营, 管理
artisan	/ˌɑːtɪˈzæn/	n.	someone who does skilled work with their hands 工匠, 手艺人

coordination	/kəʊˌɔːdɪˈneɪʃən/	n.	the organization of people or things so that they work together well 协调, 调和
spurt	/spɜːt/	n.	sudden burst of speed, effort, activity, etc. 突然加速, 劲头迸发, 活跃程度增大
bystander	/ˈbaɪˌstændə/	n.	someone who watches what is happening without taking part 旁观者
sporadic	/spəˈrædɪk/	adj.	happening in scattered and irregular instances 偶尔发生的, 零星的
work off			get rid of 除去, 消除
prestigious	/presˈtiːdʒəs/	adj.	admired as one of the best and most important 有威望的
bask	/bɑːsk/	vi.	to enjoy the approval or attention that you are getting from other people 享受（别人的恩惠、关注）
assert	/əˈsɜːt/	vt.	to state firmly that something is true 断言, 主张

Notes:

behavioral science is a term that encompasses all the disciplines that explore the activities of and interactions among organisms in the natural world.

stock broker is a qualified and regulated professional who buys and sells shares and other securities through market makers or Agency Only Firms on behalf of investors.

Reading Comprehension

I. **Summarize the text into a few sentences, which indicate the main idea of the article.**

_____
_____
_____
_____

II. **Answer the following questions.**

1. What does work offer to people?

2. Why do some people complain about their work?

3. How do you understand the essence of "Esprit de corps"?

4. Take a craftsman for example, how do people pride themselves in their accomplishments?

5. How should work be an important source of satisfaction?

III. **Judge, according to the text, whether the following statements are true or false. For false statements, write the facts in parentheses.**

1. Jobs and work do much more to provide happiness and satisfaction than most of us realize.
   (   )

2. Work is a mere necessity for most human beings, for it provides the material things of life.
   (   )

3. For many people, the absence of work does harm to their health.
   (   )

4. Relationships among people at work tend to be more complicated, and somewhat less emotional.
   (   )

5. Unemployment brings enormous psychological troubles and many individuals deteriorate rapidly when out of work.
   (   )

6. Retirement brings no problems to those who have no financial cares.
   (   )

7. Working for one of the best companies in the community provides employees with both status and self-confidence.
   (   )

IV. **Paraphrase the following sentences within the context.**

1. (Para. 1) But we are much less conscious of the extent to which work provides the more intangible, but more crucial, psychological well-being that can make the difference between a full and an empty life.

Unit 2   Jobs

2. (Para. 3) A good many patients who languish in clinics, depressed or obsessed, gain renewed self-confidence when gainfully employed and lose some, if not all, of their most acute symptoms.

_____
_____

3. (Para. 11) Not everyone can interact with such persistence and over long hours, but those who do, pride themselves on a distinctive ability that contributes mightily to the running of the organization.

_____
_____

4. (Para. 16) And the work group also gently pressures its members to learn how to adjust to one another so that the "rough edges" are worked off because people know they must do certain things with and through one another each day.

_____
_____

5. (Para. 17) We in truth bask in the reflected glory of the institution, and we seek ways of asserting our membership so that others will know and can recognize our good fortune.

_____
_____

Vocabulary Exercises

I. **Fill in the blank in each sentence with a word or phrase taken from the box in its appropriate form.**

intangible	tribute	coordination	inherent
attributable	aside from	sporadic	symptom
assert	fend for oneself		

1. The kids had to _____ while their parents were at work.
2. Weight is a(n) _____ property of matter.

3. Weight loss and fatigue are common _____ of diabetes.
4. The fall in the number of deaths from heart disease is mainly _____ to improvements in diet.
5. _____ a mild fever, the patient feels fine today.
6. The scientist _____ that nuclear power was a safe and non-polluting energy source.
7. It was a _____ to his teaching methods that so many children passed the crucial test.
8. Those agencies are working together to _____ policy on food safety.
9. The tranquility of the French countryside was almost _____.
10. The protests, blockade attempts, and arrests continued _____ for several days.

II. **Choose a word or phrase that best completes each of the following sentences.**

1. The chair was a moveable wonder—he loved the feeling of power and strength it gave him for so little _____.
   A. efforts   B. challenge   C. exertion   D. exchange
2. If you keep on taking on more work than you can do, your health will _____.
   A. degrade   B. degenerate   C. exhaust   D. deteriorate
3. His long and loyal service with the company was _____ with a present from the president.
   A. admitted   B. acknowledged   C. accomplished   D. accepted
4. The _____ of a cultural phenomenon is usually a logical consequence of some physical aspect in the life style of the people.
   A. implementation   B. expedition
   C. demonstration   D. manifestation
5. The boy's foolish question _____ his mother who was busy with housework and had no interest in talking.
   A. intrigued   B. fascinated   C. irritated   D. stimulated
6. During the flight to the Moon, Challenge I Satellite gradually _____ direction so that it can go into the programmed orbit.
   A. adjusts   B. adopts   C. adapts   D. accepts
7. Some advertisements, like the one for environmental protection, _____ to our conscience or our desire to be worthy citizens.
   A. adapt   B. attach   C. appeal   D. adjust

Unit 2　Jobs

8. —I was surprised to see wild flowers in Alaska.
   —Many people think there is nothing there _____ ice and snow.
   A. rather than   B. apart from   C. else than   D. regardless of

9. From this material we can _____ hundreds of what you may call direct products.
   A. derive   B. discern   C. diminish   D. displace

10. The final decision rests _____ the President.
    A. on   B. in   C. upon   D. with

11. He tried to _____ the public into thinking the war could still be won.
    A. deceive   B. discipline   C. disguise   D. dissuade

Translation Exercises

Translate each of the following sentences into English, using the word or phrase given in the brackets.

1. 与敌人僵持八小时后，我们做了一次战略性撤退，以积蓄力量再次进攻。(renewed)

2. 奥运圣火的点燃不只体现了"更高、更快、更强"的体育精神，还彰显了全世界多样文化的交流与融合。(more than)

3. 独立生活能力对于任何一个成年人来说都是必不可少的，所以父母应该教给孩子一些生存之道。(fend for)

4. 除了上世纪70年代约翰·丹佛所唱的几首经典歌曲外，所谓的"乡村音乐"基本上都是其他流派的歌——民歌、轻摇滚，甚至是蓝调。(aside from)

5. 香港在短短数十年间已经发展成世界重要的商业和金融中心，拥有高素质的人力资源是她成功的主要原因之一。(be attributable to)

6. 身体健康在很大程度上取决于精神健康，因此在青少年中宣传和普及心理健康知识非常重要。(in significant measure)

7. 辍学从商后，他过了很长时间才适应那种竞争激烈的环境。(adjust to)

8. 通过每天早上的锻炼，艾米成功减掉了腰围脂肪。(work off)

Text ii
Making the Best of a Good Job

Pre-reading Questions
1. Have you received an interview before? What did you think of your performance during the interview?
2. How can you make a good first impression in a job interview?

1   If your last job interview took place five or more years ago, you could be in for some big surprises when you re-enter the employment market. Interviews are now much less likely to take the form of a cosy fireside chat! Neither, at the other extreme, should you expect an intimidating interrogation supposedly designed to test your ability to cope with stress. These traditional approaches have gone the way of tea trolleys and two-hour lunch-breaks.

2   As lean modern companies have learned the costs of making bad appointments, interviews have become part of a multilayered quasi-scientific selection process, and are increasingly likely to be conducted by managers trained in complex psychological techniques. They are also becoming high tech: before too long, candidates can expect many interview panels to include at least one member who participates by means of video conferencing technology from another site or even overseas.

3   One thing has not changed. It is still unusual to get a job without a face-to-face encounter with your boss-to-be. Interviews are used by 75 per cent of companies for every category of staff they employ. The same proportion of

firms believe that, of all the selection tools available, interviews have the most influence on their appointment decisions.

But these days you cannot rely just on your skills as an interviewee to get the job you want. There is a good chance that you will have to start proving yourself well before you reach the interview room.

A recent analysis of recruitment methods by the Institute of Personnel and Development found that 61 per cent of firms also used aptitude tests, 43 per cent sent out personality questionnaires and 30 per cent evaluated potential staff at assessment centres. Professional and managerial staff are especially likely to be put through a wide range of selection techniques before they reach the final interview with the employer.

"By the time you've reached this stage, you are 90 per cent there in terms of an acceptance by the employer that you can do the job," says Bill Robbins, director of the senior executive centre at Drake Beam Morin.

"Although you may be tested further on the skills and experience the company thinks are especially important, the interview is likely to focus more on your motivation for the job and how well you will fit into the organization and its culture."

Selection panels are now putting increasing effort into probing candidates' inner values to see whether they match those of the company. Your values could even be assessed by psychological tests conducted during the interview itself.

A test devised by occupational psychology consultancy Criterion Partnership requires candidates to select, rank and then discuss cards containing value-reflecting headings or statements such as "money and status", "opportunity to make independent decisions" and "I need approval in work".

Criterion has also developed an interview exercise that assesses candidates by asking them to discuss what they believe to have been the causes of positive or negative past work experiences. Someone who is inclined to blame themselves for negative events may be judged not to have sufficient emotional stamina to take on a job dealing with customer complaints, for example.

In today's job marketplace, you can expect the interview to be a "structured" event—each candidate will be asked the same predetermined questions—rather than a process guided by whatever questions happen to float into the minds of the panel. (This standardization aims to provide a better basis for comparing candidates and reducing bias on the grounds of race or gender.) A survey found

that nine out of 10 interviews are now structured, compared with seven out of 10 two years ago.

12   An increasing number of interviews are also "situational". This means that candidates are asked questions such as "What would you do if...?", an approach that lets them provide practical examples of how they would tackle particular situations, whether or not they have had any direct experience of them.

13   Despite their increasing rigour, interviews are generally becoming a lot less formal. Candidates and interviewers are now much more likely to sit on sofas than face each other across a large mahogany table. Fran Minogue of recruitment company Norman Broadbent believes that selection panels "aim to relax people so they can open up and do as much talking as possible". This new informality also reflects the decreasing importance attached to hierarchy within organizations.

14   The biggest change in the style of interviews will be noticed by senior staff with skills currently in short supply in the labour market. "At this level, interviews are increasingly a conversation between equals", suggests Bill Robbins. "That's a big change."

15   Yet despite all efforts to bring the interview process up to date, employers frequently make the wrong choice. Although the interview remains the centrepiece of organizations' selection procedures, it is in fact a highly unreliable predictor of a candidate's suitability. When Oxford Psychologist Press examined all the evidence, they found that interviewing came third from bottom in a list of eight methods of selection. Only astrology and graphology scored worse.

16   But you would be best advised not to point this out to a potential employer —at least not until you have definitely been offered the job.

(870 words)

Reading Comprehension

I. **Answer the following questions with the information you read from the passage.**

1. What are the traditional approaches to a job interview?
2. Why do some companies adopt a multilayered quasi-scientific selection process for job interviews?

3. Is it enough for employees to rely just on skills to get the job they want? What else are needed?
4. How many kinds of job interviews are mentioned in the passage? How would you perform in these kinds of interviews?

II. Topics for discussion and reflection.
   1. What contributes to a successful job interview?
   2. What should you consider and do before looking for a job?

Exercises for Integrated Skills

I. Dictation

Listen to the following passage. Altogether the passage will be read to you four times. During the first reading, which will be read at normal speed, listen and try to understand the meaning. For the second and third readings, the passage will be read sentence by sentence, or phrase by phrase, with intervals of 15 to 20 seconds. The last reading will be done at normal speed again and during this time you should check your work. You will then be given 2 minutes to check through your work once more.

II. Cloze

Fill in the blanks in the following passage with a word or phrase taken from the box in its appropriate form.

innovate	hearty	contribute	leader	effective
tension	positive	light	suggest	assume
profitable	serious	weather	resilience	communicate

Are You Having Fun at Work?

The lack of humor in workplaces is a real shame, according to experts in corporate culture. Studies have shown that happy workers are productive workers, which enhances ___1___.

The stress that is endemic in today's workplace is no joke. If you can learn to laugh, you and everyone around you will better ___2___ the stress storms.

Paul McGhee, Ph.D., of *The Laughter Remedy* says that a good sense of humor will ___3___ to your success in these ways:

1. Change. Roles and responsibilities are changing rapidly in today's workplace. Your sense of humor provides the ___4___ needed to cope with change.

2. Growing ___5___. As your career progresses, you'll probably be asked to lead more and make more decisions in your organization. Building your humor skills will boost your ability to lead ___6___.

3. Increased stress. As already mentioned, stress is a factor in all jobs. The more responsibility you ___7___, the more stress you experience. Humor is one of the most powerful stress-management tools around. Laughter helps you reduce muscle ___8___, release anger, improve your ability to overcome panic and bring anxiety under control, as well as keep a more ___9___ frame of mind.

4. Demand for creativity and ___10___. A better sense of humor will enhance your creative thinking abilities.

5. Outstanding ___11___ skills. Everyone in your organization needs these skills, and humor can be a wonderful way both to boost interest in what you have to say and help you become an accepted team member.

Okay, are you ready to laugh it up and encourage your colleagues to do the same? Here are several helpful ___12___ to get you started using humor.

Step 1. Surround yourself with humor and determine the nature of your sense of humor. How to do this? Watch more comedy movies; look for cartoons in magazines and newspapers; spend more time with your funniest friends and colleagues. Step 2. Become more playful and overcome ___13___. Spend more time playing with your kids; make a list of things you find fun and do one of them every day. Step 3. Laugh more ___14___ and start telling jokes. Step 4. Play language, puns, and other verbal games. Step 5. Find humor in everyday life. Look for the unexpected, incongruous, bizarre, and ridiculous aspects of life. Step 6. Take yourself ___15___; laugh at your own mistakes. Step 7. Find humor in the midst of stress.

Unit 2 Jobs

Oral Activities

Activity One: Work in groups and discuss the following questions.

1. In your opinion, what is an ideal job like?
2. In order to meet challenges in the future, what do you think college students should do?
3. What is the most crucial factor in a successful job hunting? Do you favor "study in work" or "work after study"?

Activity Two: A Simulated Job Interview

The class is to be divided into two groups. Representatives from Group 1 act as employers seeking to hire employees. Representatives from Group 2 act as college students seeking part-time jobs. Now, start the interview. After it, the employers should fill in the "Job Interview Rating Sheet" and decide who they would like to hire.

Job Interview Rating Sheet

Name(s) of Participant(s) _____

INSTRUCTIONS: Fill in the correct score bubble. Comments should help participants identify their strengths and areas for improvement.

Key To Scoring

Very High (5)	High (4)	Medium (3)
Low (2)	Very Low (1)	Not Evident (0)

Criteria	Score				
Appearance	①	②	③	④	⑤
Communication skills	①	②	③	④	⑤
Knowledge of job	①	②	③	④	⑤
Problem solving	①	②	③	④	⑤
Skills needed	①	②	③	④	⑤
Creativity	①	②	③	④	⑤
Aggressive but thoughtful	①	②	③	④	⑤
Overall Evaluation	①	②	③	④	⑤

General Comments:

_____

_____

Interviewed by: _____

Signature: _____   Date: _____

Writing Practice

Note Writing: A Note of Congratulation

Write a note to your friend, Mary, to congratulate her on passing the preliminary test and several rounds of interviews and finally receiving a job offer from the IBM Company.

>   10 March, 20 ____
> Dear Mary,
>
>
>
>
>   With love,

Composition Writing

What kind of job do you want to have, a non-challenging job with much leisure time, or a high-stress one with a considerable salary? Write a composition of about 120 words about your choice. The reasons for your choice should be included in the composition.

Unit 3 Business

Warm-up Activities

1. Nowadays, a great number of students do business while attending university. Some even drop out of college to start a business. What is your view towards this phenomenon? What are the pros and cons?
2. What do you do with your extra money? Do you prefer to save it or spend it? Do you have any investment plans?

Text I

Japanese Style in Decision-Making

Pre-reading Questions

1. How do you make important decisions? How does your way of making decisions differ from that of your friends? What contributes to the differences?
2. It is a crucial business skill to be able to negotiate effectively. What traits make an effective negotiator in international business?

1 To talk about problem-solving or decision-making within a national environment means examining many complex cultural forces. It means trying to measure the impact of these forces on contemporary life, and also coming to grips with changes now taking place. It also means using dangerous comparisons—and the need to translate certain fundamental concepts which resist translation and comparisons.

2   For example, the concept of vocational or professional identity differs markedly between the United States and Japan. In the West, the emphasis is on what a man or woman does for a living. In the U.S., if you ask a boy what his father does, he will say "My daddy drives a truck" or "My daddy is a stock broker" or "My daddy is an engineer." But in Japan, the boy will tell you "My daddy works for Mitsubishi" or "My daddy works for Nomura Securities" or for "Hitachi." But you will have no idea whether his father is President of Hitachi or a chauffeur at Hitachi.

3   In Japan, the most important thing is what organization you work for. This becomes very significant when you try to analyze the direction-taking or decision-making process. At the least, it explains the greater job stability in Japan, in contrast to the great job mobility in America. While we differ in many ways, such differences are neither superior nor inferior to each other. A particular pattern of management behavior develops from a complexity of unique cultural factors—and will only work within a given culture. Let me try to describe three or four characteristics of the Japanese environment that in some way affect decision-making or direction-taking and problem-solving. These characteristics are interrelated.

4   First, in any approach to a problem and in any negotiations in Japan, there is the "you to you" approach, as distinguished from the Western "I to you" approach. The difference is this: in "I to you," each side presents his arguments forthrightly from his own point of view—he states what he wants and what he expects to get. Thus, a confrontation situation is set up, and Westerners are very adroit in dealing with this. The "you to you" approach practiced in Japan is based on each side—automatically and often unconsciously—trying to understand the other man's point of view, and for the purpose of the discussion actually declaring this understanding. Thus, the direction of the meeting is a mutual attempt at minimizing confrontation and achieving harmony.

5   A second characteristic is based on "consensus opinion" and "bottom-up direction". In Japan great consideration is given to and great reliance is placed

on the thoughts and opinions of everyone at all levels. This is true of corporate enterprises and government agencies. To understand this, it is important to realize that Japan is a very densely populated homogeneous country. Moreover, the people are aware and are articulate. Literacy is almost 100 per cent. Problems are shared. In Japan there is a drive for the group—whether it is the family, company, or government—to act as a unit.

6   Tremendous weight is given to the achievement of solidarity and unanimity. Unilateral decision-making or direction-taking is generally avoided, or where it does occur for very practical urgent reasons, it usually happens along with a sounding out of all concerned.

7   This brings us to the second part of this characteristic. When I use the term "bottom-up," I am referring to a style of management—perhaps what you would call keeping your finger on the pulse of the public, or the labor force, or other audiences. The difference is that in Japan we record the pulse and it has real meaning, and it influences the direction finally taken at the top regarding a specific important issue. In other words, Western style decision-making proceeds predominantly from top management and often does not consult middle management or the worker, while in Japan, direction can be formulated at the lowest levels, travel upward through an organization and have an impact on the eventual decision. This is "bottom up".

8   There is also a characteristic style of communication in Japan that is different from the Western way. The Japanese businessman works to achieve harmony, even if the deal falls through, and he will spend whatever time is necessary to determine his "you to you" approach and he will communicate his own views indirectly and with great sensitivity.

9   This places time in a different perspective. In Japan the Western deadline approach is secondary to a thorough job. The Japanese are thorough in their meetings as well as in their production. Thus Americans are often exasperated by the seemingly endless sequences of meetings of many Japanese businessmen. But where Americans are pressing for a specific decision, the Japanese are trying to formulate a rather broad direction. On the other hand, once agreement is established, it is the Japanese who sometimes wonder at the leisurely pace of execution by Westerners. The Japanese are eager for execution and Westerners, perhaps, like to take the time for in-depth planning. Now, while Japan's industry and technology are highly developed, they have not replaced the fundamental

force of human energy and motivation. By that I mean that the Japanese take great pride in doing a job well and getting it done no matter how much time is required.

10   There is a dedication and sense of responsibility which have not been replaced by the machine age. Perhaps we are not so sophisticated yet. In my field—finance and securities—I am often asked by Westerners how Nomura Securities has managed to escape the paper logjam that American brokerage firms have faced. We, too, have had that problem.

11   The Tokyo Stock Exchange often has a turnover of between 200 and 300 million shares a day. This volume is many times more than that of the New York Stock Exchange. How can we possibly handle this load?

12   First, we have very advanced computerization. Second, and most important, the personnel responsible for processing all these transactions stay and stay till all hours until the job is done. And their families understand that this is something that they must do, for the survival and progress of the company and for their own mutual security as well. Perhaps in 20 years—or sooner—they will be more Westernized and insist on going home at five o'clock. But today, still, most insist on staying until the job is done. There is concern for workmanship. This willingness to pitch in is an important aspect of Japanese problem-solving, and you find it at every level.

13   Some years ago, the Matsushita Company was having a very bad time. Among the many measures taken, Mr. Matsushita, the founder and then chairman, became the manager of the sales department. Also, when we at Nomura converted to computers about five years ago, the new system eliminated the jobs of 700 bookkeepers and accountants who were using abacuses. We got rid of the abacuses but we did not get rid of the people. We converted our bookkeepers and accountants to securities salesmen and some of these today are our leading salespeople.

14   Where there is willingness and intelligence, there is a place within the company to try and succeed. In Japan, a person's capabilities are not forced into an inflexible specialty. And we feel the company owes him something for his loyalty and commitment.

(1,217 words)

Words and Expressions

impact	/'ɪmpækt/	n.	the effect or influence that an event, situation, etc. has on someone or something 影响，作用
come to grips with something			to make an effort to understand and deal with a problem or situation 了解并应对（难题或局面）
comparison	/kəm'pærɪsən/	n.	the process of comparing two or more people or things 比较
vocational identity			职业认同
professional identity			专业认同
marked	/mɑːkt/	adj.	very easy to notice 明显的，显著的 **markedly** adv. 明显地，显著地
emphasis	/'emfəsɪs/	n.	special attention or importance 重点
chauffeur	/'ʃəʊfə/	n.	someone whose job is to drive a car for a rich or important person（为他人开车的）司机
stability	/stə'bɪlɪtɪ/	n.	the condition of being steady and not changing 稳定
in contrast to			相比之下，与……相反
mobility	/məʊ'bɪlɪtɪ/	n.	the ability to move easily from one job, area, or social class to another 易变性，流动性
inferior	/ɪn'fɪərɪə/	adj.	not good, or not as good as someone or something else 差的，次的
complexity	/kəm'pleksɪtɪ/	n.	the state of being complicated 复杂性，错综复杂
interrelated	/ɪntərɪ'leɪtɪd/	adj.	being connected and having an effect on each other 相互关联的，相互影响的
negotiation	/nɪˌgəʊʃɪ'eɪʃən/	n.	official discussions between the representatives of opposing groups who are trying to reach an agreement, especially in business or politics 谈判，协商
forthright	/'fɔːθ'raɪt/	adj.	too honest and direct 直截了当的 **forthrightly** adv. 直截了当地
confrontation	/ˌkɒnfrʌn'teɪʃən/	n.	a situation in which there is a lot of angry disagreements between two people or groups 对抗，冲突
adroit	/ə'drɔɪt/	adj.	clever and skilful, especially in the way you

			use words and arguments 机敏的,灵巧的
mutual	/ˈmjuːtjʊəl/	adj.	(of two or more people or groups) feeling the same emotion, or doing the same thing to or for each other 相互的,彼此的
minimize	/ˈmɪnɪmaɪz/	vt.	to reduce something that is difficult, dangerous, or unpleasant to the smallest possible amount or degree 把……减至最小量(最低程度)
densely populated			with a lot of people living close together in the same area 人口稠密的
homogeneous	/ˌhɒməʊˈdʒiːnjəs/	adj.	consisting of people or things that are all of the same type 由同种族人或同类事物组成的
articulate	/ɑːˈtɪkjʊlɪt/	adj.	able to talk easily and effectively about things, especially difficult subjects 能清楚表达的
literacy	/ˈlɪtərəsɪ/	n.	the state of being able to read and write 有文化,有读写能力
drive	/draɪv/	n.	an effort to achieve something (为实现某事而进行的)努力
solidarity	/ˌsɒlɪˈdærɪtɪ/	n.	agreement between and support for the members of a group, especially a political group 团结,一致
unanimity	/ˌjuːnəˈnɪmɪtɪ/	n.	a state or situation of complete agreement among a group of people 一致同意
unilateral	/ˌjuːnɪˈlætərəl/	adj.	involving only one group or country 单方面的,单边的
proceed	/prəˈsiːd/	vi.	to continue to do something that has already been planned or started 继续进行
predominantly	/prɪˈdɒmɪnəntlɪ/	adv.	mostly or mainly 主要地,绝大多数地
formulate	/ˈfɔːmjʊleɪt/	vt.	to develop all the details of a plan for doing something 制定,构想
eventual	/ɪˈventjʊəl/	adj.	happening at the end of a long period of time or after a lot of other things have happened 最后发生的,最终获得的
fall through			fail utterly; collapse 失败,化为泡影
sensitivity	/ˌsensɪˈtɪvɪtɪ/	n.	the ability to understand other people's feelings and problems 理解
secondary	/ˈsekəndərɪ/	adj.	being of second rank or importance or value 第二位的,次要的

Unit 3 Business

exasperate	/ɪgˈzɑːspəreɪt/	vt.	to make someone very annoyed by continuing to do something that upsets them 使恼怒
seemingly	/ˈsiːmɪŋli/	adv.	appearing to have a particular quality, when this may or may not be true 表面上，看上去
sequence	/ˈsiːkwəns/	n.	a series of related events, actions, etc. that happen or are done in a particular order 一连串
execution	/ˌeksɪˈkjuːʃən/	n.	when something is done or performed, especially in a planned way 执行，实施
in-depth	/ˈɪnˈdepθ/	adj.	thorough, complete, and considering all the details 深入的，彻底的
dedication	/ˌdedɪˈkeɪʃən/	n.	hard work or effort that someone puts into a particular activity because they care about it a lot 敬业精神
sophisticated	/səˈfɪstɪkeɪtɪd/	adj.	having a lot of knowledge and experience in difficult or complicated subjects and therefore able to understand them well 富有经验的，老练的
logjam	/ˈlɒgdʒæm/	n.	a situation in which a lot of problems are preventing progress from being made 僵局，阻碍
brokerage firm			经纪行
stock exchange			证券交易所
turnover	/ˈtɜːnˌəʊvə/	n.	the amount of business done during a particular period 成交量
share	/ʃeə/	n.	one of the equal parts into which the ownership of a company is divided and which can be bought by members of the public 股，股份
volume	/ˈvɒljuːm/	n.	the total amount of something, especially when it is large or increasing 总量
computerize	/kəmˈpjuːtəraɪz/	vt.	to use a computer to control the way something is done, to store information, etc. 计算机化 **computerization** n. 计算机的使用
transaction	/trænˈzækʃən/	n.	a business deal (一笔)交易
survival	/səˈvaɪvəl/	n.	the state of continuing to live or exist 继续生存，幸存
westernize	/ˈwestənaɪz/	vt.	to bring customs, business methods, etc. that

			are typical of Europe and the U.S. to other countries 使(风俗、经营方式等)西化
workmanship	/'wɜːkmənʃɪp/	n.	skill in making things, especially in a way that makes them look good 工艺,手艺
pitch in			开始大干特干
eliminate	/ɪ'lɪmɪneɪt/	vt.	to completely get rid of something that is unnecessary or unwanted 消除,根除
bookkeeper	/'bʊkˌkiːpə/	n.	someone whose job is to record the financial accounts of an organization 会计
abacus	/'æbəkəs/	n.	a wooden frame with small beads used for counting 算盘
specialty	/'speʃəltɪ/	n.	a subject or job that you know a lot about or have a lot of experience in 专业,专长
loyalty	/'lɔɪəltɪ/	n.	the quality of remaining faithful to your friends, principles, country, etc. 忠心,忠诚

Notes:

Mitsubishi Mitsubishi Companies is a Japanese conglomerate consisting of a range of autonomous businesses which share the Mitsubishi brand, trademark and legacy. The first Mitsubishi company was a shipping firm established in 1870. Now, it engages in business with customers around the world in many industries.

Nomura Securities is a wholly owned subsidiary of Nomura Holdings, Inc. It plays a central role in the securities business. Established in 1925 in Osaka, it is the oldest brokerage firm in Japan.

Hitachi, Ltd. is a multinational corporation specializing in high-technology and services. Hitachi was founded in 1910 as an electrical repair shop. Today, it is one of the leading manufacturers in new technology.

Reading Comprehension

I. **Put the following items in the appropriate category.**

    A. My daddy works for IBM.   B. My mommy is an engineer.
    C. "I to you" approach   D. "you to you" approach
    E. pressing for a specific decision   F. formulating a broad direction
    G. adroit in dealing with confrontation   H. "consensus opinion"

Japanese style: _____
Western style: _____

II. **Answer the following questions.**
   1. How do you understand the "complex cultural forces" in decision-making?
   2. What is the difference between the Japanese and Americans in interpreting their professional identities?
   3. What are the Japanese characteristics that influence their decision-making?
   4. What does the term "bottom-up" mean in business management?
   5. How did Nomura Securities manage to escape the paper logjam?

III. **Judge, according to the text, whether the following statements are true or false. For false statements, write the facts in parentheses.**
   1. The concept of professional identity in Japan is very similar to America's concept of vocational identity.
      (   )
   2. The differences between Americans and Japanese are either superior or inferior to each other.
      (   )
   3. Great consideration is given to and great reliance is placed on the thoughts and opinions of everyone at all levels in Japan.
      (   )
   4. In the "you to you" approach, each side presents his arguments directly from his own point of view.
      (   )
   5. In Japan the Western deadline approach is secondary to a thorough job.
      (   )
   6. Japanese industry and technology are so highly developed that they have replaced the force of human energy and motivation.
      (   )

IV. **Paraphrase the following sentences within the context.**
   1. (Para. 1) It means trying to measure the impact of these forces on contemporary life, and also coming to grips with changes now taking place.

2. (Para. 4) Thus, a confrontation situation is set up, and Westerners are very adroit in dealing with this.

3. (Para. 6) Tremendous weight is given to the achievement of solidarity and unanimity.

4. (Para. 7) The difference is that in Japan we record the pulse and it has real meaning, and it influences the direction finally taken at the top regarding a specific important issue.

5. (Para. 9) But where Americans are pressing for a specific decision, the Japanese are trying to formulate a rather broad direction.

6. (Para. 13) Also, when we at Nomura converted to computers about five years ago, the new system eliminated the jobs of 700 bookkeepers and accountants who were using abacuses.

Vocabulary Exercises

I. **Fill in each blank with one of the given words and note the difference of meaning between them. Change the form when necessary.**
   1. TREMENDOUS   IMMENSE
      a. Setting off firecrackers makes a(n) _____ noise and causes serious air pollution.

b. As a great many people are to visit the country, the government will build new hotels, a(n) _____ stadium and a new Olympic standard swimming pool.

c. The plane is travelling at a(n) _____ speed.

d. The ship hit herself on a(n) _____ iceberg and sank into the sea.

e. This plan could save us a(n) _____ amount of money.

2. SOPHISTICATED   COMPLICATED

a. For young kids, getting dressed is a _____ matter.

b. Although she is only 16, Sophia is quite _____ and witty.

c. Mental illness is a highly _____ subject.

d. After two years' research, they finally worked out a highly _____ weapons system.

II. Fill in the blank in each sentence with a word or phrase taken from the box in its appropriate form.

inflexible	press for	forthrightly	solidarity
come to grips with	execution	exasperate	unanimity
formulate	predominantly		

1. We must continue to _____ a solution to the problem.
2. People were _____ in support of the peace effort.
3. We will effectively strengthen the _____ and cooperation with developing nations.
4. In his paintings, the _____ color is black.
5. She answered the President's question in her usual _____ manner.
6. It was my grandfather who _____ the Labour Party's education policy in 1922.
7. So far the government has not _____ the economic problem.
8. The job involves drawing up and _____ a plan of nursing care.
9. The government needs a more _____ approach to education.
10. It _____ me that they never kept their promises.

III. Choose a word or phrase that best completes each of the following sentences.

1. With the introduction of _____ technology, information flows faster than it ever has.
   A. involved   B. complicated   C. sophisticated   D. complex

2. The studio planned to make a movie of the book but the deal _____.
   A. fell through   B. fell down   C. fell off   D. fell behind

3. After dinner, they all pitched _____ and finished the work within two hours.
   A. up   B. in   C. to   D. into

4. Some educators try to put students of similar abilities into the same class because they believe this kind of _____ grouping is beneficial.
   A. harmonious   B. spontaneous
   C. instantaneous   D. homogeneous

5. It will be safer to walk the streets because people will not need to carry large amounts of cash; virtually all financial _____ will be conducted by computer.
   A. transactions   B. transitions
   C. transmissions   D. transformations

Translation Exercises

Translate the following sentences into English, using the word or phrase given in the brackets.

1. 这件鲜绿色宽松长袍与她乌黑的直发形成了鲜明对比。(in contrast to)

2. 经理身材瘦小，有点内向，对大家很恭敬，从外表上丝毫看不出他与职员们有什么不同。(distinguish from)

3. 不论朋友、恋人、同事、家人，信任是建立良好人际关系最重要的基石。(set up)

4. 他善于使事态向有利于他的方向发展，并且还有当机立断之才。(be adroit in)

5. 他本来计划八月前为灾区儿童建三所希望小学，但由于资金短缺，计划失败了。(fall through)

6. 汶川大地震发生后，我们首先考虑的是人民群众的安全，其他都是次要的。(be secondary to)

7. 虽然存在种种顾虑，但白宫官员坚持说，布什总统已经下定决心在今年推行社会保障制度改革。(press for)

8. 虽然工作环境很糟糕，但如果我们都出一份力，就肯定能在今天下午完成这项任务。(pitch in)

Text II

Playing to Win

Pre-reading Questions

1. What sports activities do you like to take part in? Do you play to entertain or play to win?
2. If you were a professional athlete, what would you expect from the games?

1   The need for professional sports management has never been greater. In order to raise their game, many clubs and sporting bodies have been turning to business schools to help them develop leadership skills. But businesses can also learn a lot from the motivational techniques employed by sports coaches. It is a two-way process.

2   John Neal runs the Sports Business Initiative at Ashridge Business School, a study centre where sports coaches and MBA students learn the techniques of leadership side by side. A sports psychologist, Neal has spent 20 years coaching at Middlesex Cricket Club, Somerset, and with the England rugby team. He

came to Ashridge five years ago to teach stress-management techniques to MBA students, helping them to manage their revision time ahead of their exams.

3   He set up the Sports Business Initiative in 2002, a year before England won the Rugby World Cup, and discovered that sport and business had a lot to learn from each other. Neal says, "Sport and business are both about people, process, teamwork and leadership. Sport is very good at one-to-one inspiration and motivation; business is about achieving results. It is performance-based."

4   Ashridge's Sports Business Initiative features a brand of appraisal adapted from classic management theory and based on 10 key competencies that apply to business and sport. Neal says, "The object of the appraisal is to build up a picture of how your peers see you before putting together a personal development programme. In sport we really clarify personal objectives—what a player needs to do to help win the game. In business we rarely do that."

5   The Sports Business Initiative began by running training for top-level sports coaches half a day a week in partnership with the English and Welsh Rugby Board. Last year, Ashridge signed a deal with the British Olympic Association to train 30–40 sports coaches a year up to the 2012 Olympics. They join the same open programme as MBA students on its one-year, full-time MBA. Neal says, "The British Olympic Association has vowed Britain will be the fourth in the medal's table. We are aiming to give our coaches the edge."

6   Neal has borrowed techniques of target setting and appraisal from business and applied them to sports. In turn, business students are learning to raise their game from the intense results-driven focus of competitive sport.

7   Richard Hill, the head coach for Bristol Rugby Club, is coming to the end of his Ashridge course. He found that business people in the MBA course were fascinated by the techniques he used. Hill says, "Business people were staggered at how much feedback we give to players. Before a match we seat each one down in front of a laptop and go through each person's aims and objectives and what their peers have said about their previous game. It's called the "90-minute preview/review".

8   Hill also claims to have picked up some very good ideas from business

about how a line manager sets targets with employees. He says, "We now set targets—ask each player personal aims—such as their target weight, upper and lower body strength, flexibility and endurance."

9   Players are finding that the more feedback they are given, the more they value the process and the more open they become to change. Hill observes, "In the business world I've discovered people are frightened to death about going in for an appraisal with their line manager, but my players are now demanding feedback. Getting your teammates together to comment on your performance during the match is a real team-building, confidence-building exercise. It has to be tackled within 24 hours of playing while the memories are still fresh in the mind. And because everyone participates, we all learn from it and we learn to trust one another."

10   Lack of blame is crucial and player feedback will contribute towards putting together a set of tactics that might win the next game. Hill also asked the players to give him feedback on his coaching—a brave move. "I found I was good in certain areas like communicating instructions but I was not doing so well in terms of emotional intelligence. Knowing the players better will help me understand when to apply the pressure and when to relax a little."

11   The MBA programme at the University of Bath Business School also makes the link between sport and business. Bath, along with Loughborough University, is one of the only two world-class centres for sports studies and sporting excellence in the UK. Peggy Van Luyn, director of MBA programmes, says, "At first it was running wellness programmes for MBA students—training them in the best ways to relax, and to achieve more from their studies. Now we are starting to attract more students from sports management who come to complete their MBA part-time."

12   As at Ashridge, collaboration works both ways. Team Bath, the commercial arm of the university's sports science and coaching courses, is borrowing from business best practice. Says Director Nicky Fossey-Lewis, "Ten years ago, athletes would have been encouraged to train all the hours God sends. Now, like business, it is quality not quantity that counts. We look at time management, rest and recovery and healthy eating—all the things that influence performance whether on the athletics track or in the office."

(881 words)

Reading Comprehension

I. Answer the following questions with the information you read from the passage.

1. What does "a two-way process" in the first paragraph imply?
2. What is the "Sports Business Initiative" according to the implication of the passage?
3. Why does John Neal think "sport and business had a lot to learn from each other"?
4. What is the object of the appraisal featuring Ashridge's Sports Business Initiative? Is it practical? Why or why not?

II. Topics for discussion and reflection.

1. Do you think it viable for Britain to win more medals in the 2012 Olympics if more sports coaches are sent to Ashridge for the MBA Programme? Why or why not?
2. What can the business world and the sporting world learn from each other?

Exercises for Integrated Skills

I. Dictation

  Listen to the following passage. Altogether the passage will be read to you four times. During the first reading, which will be read at normal speed, listen and try to understand the meaning. For the second and third readings, the passage will be read sentence by sentence, or phrase by phrase, with intervals of 15 to 20 seconds. The last reading will be done at normal speed again and during this time you should check your work. You will then be given 2 minutes to check through your work once more.

Unit 3 Business

II. **Cloze**

Fill in each blank in the passage below with a word taken from the box in its appropriate form.

> commercial   impact   launch   giant   community
> campaign   athlete   innovate   craft   define
> download   beyond   globe   monitor   recognize

Few companies ___1___ 20th century marketing better than Nike. The ___2___ shoemaker's famous swoosh emblem and a string of ad ___3___, starting with its iconic "Just Do It" series, set the gold standard for getting a clear message to a mass audience. But when Nike ___4___ its World Cup strategy, it decided to try something new: online ___5___. The centerpiece was Joga.com, a social networking site for soccer fans. It was quietly ___6___ in February with Google. Members in 140 countries can blog, create fan communities around their favorite teams or players, such as Brazilian superstar Ronaldinho, organize pickup games, ___7___ videos, and rant against the encroaching ___8___ of the game. And though the program was launched during the World Cup, it continues ___9___ the tournament.

It's a huge U-turn for the mighty marketer—and a ___10___ that it needs to get consumers' attention in entirely new ways beyond blasting top-down mass messages. Nike was forced to be ___11___ after its rival Adidas Group got a World Cup exclusive deal to broadcast ads in the U.S. But by ___12___ conversations on social networking sites and blogs, where people are already shaping Nike's brand, the sneaker ___13___ knew this was an opportunity to try something different. Says Trevor Edwards, Nike's vice-president for ___14___ brand management: "Gone are the days of the one big ad, the one big shoe, and the hope that when we put it all together it makes a big ___15___."

Oral Activities

Activity One: Dialogues

Make dialogues based on the following situations:

1. You are a manager of an IT company, and you receive a call from the CEO of Motorola asking for some information about your company.
2. The CEO comes to your company for a visit. You are going to introduce your company and show him around.
3. The CEO is quite satisfied with your company's latest product, and decides that your company is to be the OEM (Original Equipment Manufacturer) of the product for Motorola. Negotiate the terms and conditions with him.

Activity Two: Team Project

Divide the class into teams of 4 or 5. Each team is to set up a sports company and prepare a presentation with the following guidelines:

1. Give a name to your company.
2. State specifically the company's vision, corporate structure, core values as well as senior management.
3. Introduce the company's competitive advantages over the other companies (such as brand, distribution network, research and development).
4. Introduce the company's featured products.

Writing Practice

Letter Writing: A Letter of Inquiry

Susanna hopes to expand her business to franchise the symbolic products of the Shanghai World Expo. Help Susanna write a formal letter to the Bureau of Shanghai World Expo Coordination, asking for qualifications and other related policies.

Sender's Address
Date
Inside Address

Dear Sir/Madam,

Sincerely yours,
Susanna Price
Sales Manager
XX Company

Composition Writing

    Competition is a way of life in today's world. We witness competitions not only in business alone, but also in many other forms such as the Olympic Games, college entrance examinations and presidential elections. Cooperation, as many people think, kills the spirit of competition.

    What is your view on the relationship between competition and cooperation? Which do you think is more important? Write a composition to express your view within 120 words.

Unit 4 Music

Warm-up Activities

1. Describe the different emotions that you experience while listening to different genres of music.
2. Be a Music Therapist
   Suppose you are a music therapist and have been asked to help three people who have physical or mental problems. What songs or musical pieces are you going to play to help them out? The following is some information about the three patients.
   Patient 1: a 21-year-old boy with lung cancer. He has only 3 months left to live.
   Patient 2: a girl who was dumped by her boyfriend and is depressed.
   Patient 3: a white-collar worker constantly under pressure. He is suffering insomnia.

Text I

Music and Healing

Pre-reading Questions

1. Music means different to different people. What roles does music play in your daily life?
2. How does music affect your body, behavior and spirit? Did it once heal your body, strengthen your mind or unlock your creative spirit?

1 Ignoring the power of music and sound and its profound effects on us can be not only unhealthy, but dangerous. Psychologist Roberto Assagioli, author of *Psychosynthesis*, believes music can facilitate the development of our highest potential as human beings or it can plunge us into despair and depression and even cause disease.

2 Music is this powerful because much of our response to it occurs below the level of consciousness. We are usually not aware that our pulse speeds up with the rhythm of a certain piece of music, or that a certain melodic pattern may trigger the memory of an open field we used to play in as children.

3 Although our responses to music may not come up into conscious awareness, they still affect us subconsciously. Because the images that arise from the music do not involve critical analysis, they are absorbed automatically and directly. As a result, they penetrate much more deeply into our consciousness. We might suddenly feel frazzled or tense, tearful or playful, without ever knowing what brought on those feelings.

4 Unless we begin to notice what the music we listen to is doing to our bodies, our brains, our psyches, and our spirits, we can easily let ourselves be manipulated by it. Advertisers have long known and understood the power of music, and they use it to persuade customers to buy their products.

5 Lately, they seem to have become quite knowledgeable about classical music, using it wisely and well. A commercial for a computer, for example, appropriately uses a Bach two-part invention. The precise, highly organized structure of this music focuses the mind and is a bridge to the highly ordered world of the computer. The Tchaikovsky Violin Concerto or a Brahms symphony simply would not be as fitting. Unconsciously, the right music creates an affinity with the product that we would not consciously choose.

6 Music has this much influence on our lives for a very good reason: we are music. We live and breathe in sound. Not only do we live in it, but it lives in us as well. At any given moment, your body could be responding to many different

sounds simultaneously without your ever knowing it: the hum of your refrigerator, the beeping and screeching of traffic noises through the window, the sputtering of a neighbor's lawn mower—as well as the soothing strains of a violin concerto flowing out of your radio. Since our physical bodies are resonators, we are always responding to the vibrational patterns around us.

7   Long ago, music was used as a therapeutic tool for balance and harmony. The ancients knew, by way of "direct knowing" or intuition, the significance of music and sound. It was understood that illness was not just a physical phenomenon. For example, it is said that the ancient Chinese emperors would send wise men to visit villages and listen to the music being played. By noting how close the sounds came to the ancient Chinese pitch, the emperor would determine whether there would be war or peace, plenty or pestilence. The music was an indicator of the economic and political condition of the village.

8   Confucius believed that music had a great influence on the mental state and therefore the political and psychological ambience of a whole nation. He wrote:

When a somber and depressing type of music prevails, we know the people are distressed and sorrowful. When a languorous, easy type of music with many long-drawn-out airs prevail, we know the people are peaceful and happy. When a strong and forceful type of music prevails, beginning with a full display of sounds, we know that the people are hearty and strong. When a pure, pious, and majestic type of music prevails, we know that the people are pious; when a gentle, lucid and quietly progressing type of music prevails, we know that the people are kind and affectionate. When lewd, exciting and upsetting music prevails, we know that the people are immoral. When the climate deteriorates, animal and plant life degenerate, and when the world is chaotic, the rituals and music become licentious. We find then a type of music that is rueful without restraint and joyous without calm. Therefore, the superior man tries to create harmony in the human heart by a rediscovery of human nature, and tries to promote music as a means to the perfection of human culture. When such music prevails and the people's minds are led toward the right ideals and aspirations, we may see the appearance of a great nation.

9   The ancient Greeks, as well, had great respect for music. Pythagoras under-

stood what classroom teachers are now realizing: that certain sequences of chords can actually change behavior. He saw the universe as a musical instrument. He believed in a cosmic vibration that could enter the being through the mind. One in tune with this cosmic vibration was a healthy person.

10   These vibrations cannot be consciously heard; they may include grass growing or the sun moving across the sky or the stars twinkling. But we are affected by them nevertheless. When we feel irritable or out-of-sorts, we are likely to be out of tune with this cosmic vibration. When things feel just right, there is a deep knowing that we are aligned to it. Often people feel that alignment when they are surrounded by nature's beauty, or even imagining a nature scene in their minds.

11   As we become aware of what inner harmony feels like, we also become more aware of the uncomfortable tension of disharmony and discord within us. With our growing sensitivity to these vibrations, we begin to choose the harmonious in our lives and avoid the discord that isolates us from our natural universe. Pythagoras advised people to begin and end each day with music. He claimed it liberates the listener from the day's conflicts and concerns and enables him or her to sleep more soundly and dream more vividly.

12   We rarely think about what we listen to when we go to sleep in the evening and much less about what we awaken to in the morning. News of world disasters, hard rock, and endless commercial jingles assail our ears. We take them into our bodies and psyches without really understanding how deeply they affect us. Try using classical music to begin and end your day—and notice the difference.

13   I often wake up to Haydn string quartets. They get me out of bed gently with their stimulating energy. People who are not "morning people" may feel a little too stimulated with these. A cassette tape recommended by Linda Keiser for attuning to the day is *Morning Moods* by Deutsche Gramophon. The selection from Grieg's *Peer Gynt Suite*, also called "Morning Mood," feels like slow stretching, or the sun gradually rising. The Mozart *Flute and Harp Concerto*, especially the slow movement, usually lulls me to sleep.

14   Since the response to music is very personal, these pieces may have a different effect on you, but the experience will broaden your sensitivity to the different ways music can make you feel.

(1,174 words)

Words and Expressions

profound	/prəˈfaʊnd/	adj.	having a strong influence or effect（影响）深远的
facilitate	/fəˈsɪlɪteɪt/	vt.	to make it easier for a process or activity to happen 有助于,使容易
plunge	/plʌndʒ/	vt.	to suddenly put someone or something into bad situation（突然）使（某人或某物）陷入糟糕的情形
rhythm	/ˈrɪðəm/	n.	a regular repeated pattern of sounds or movements 节奏
melodic	/mɪˈlɒdɪk/	adj.	concerned with the main tune in a piece of music 旋律的
trigger	/ˈtrɪgə/	vt.	to make something happen very quickly 激发,引发
subconscious	/ˈsʌbˈkɒnʃəs/	adj.	hidden in your mind and affecting your behaviour, without your awareness 下意识的,潜意识的 **subconsciously** adv. 下意识地,潜意识地
penetrate	/ˈpenɪtreɪt/	vi.	to move into or through something 进入,渗入
frazzled	/ˈfræzəld/	adj.	feeling tired and anxious 疲惫不堪的
playful	/ˈpleɪfəl/	adj.	very active, happy, and wanting to have fun 开心的
psyche	/ˈsaɪkɪ/	n.	someone's mind, or their deepest feelings, which control their attitudes and behaviour 精神,心灵
manipulate	/məˈnɪpjʊleɪt/	vt.	to control something or someone to your advantage 操纵,控制
advertiser	/ˈædvətaɪzə/	n.	a person who advertises 登广告者
commercial	/kəˈmɜːʃəl/	n.	an advertisement on television or radio 商业广告
two-part invention			二部创意曲
concerto	/kənˈtʃɜːtəʊ/	n.	a piece of classical music, usually for one instrument and an orchestra 协奏曲
symphony	/ˈsɪmfənɪ/	n.	a long piece of music usually in four parts, written for an orchestra 交响乐
fitting	/ˈfɪtɪŋ/	adj.	right for a particular situation or occasion 合适的
affinity	/əˈfɪnɪtɪ/	n.	strong liking for or attraction to somebody or something 喜爱
simultaneous	/ˌsɪməlˈteɪnɪəs/	adj.	happening at exactly the same time 同时的
hum	/hʌm/	n.	a low continuous sound 嗡嗡声
beep	/biːp/	vi.	to make a short loud sound 嘟嘟响
screech	/skriːtʃ/	vi.	to make a loud high noise 发出刺耳的声音

Unit 4 Music

sputter	/ˈspʌtə/	vi.	to make short soft uneven noise like very small explosions 噼啪作声
lawn mower			a machine for cutting grass 割草机
soothing	/ˈsuːðɪŋ/	adj.	making people feel calmer and less anxious, upset, or angry 令人舒畅的，抚慰的
strain	/streɪn/	n.	the sound of music being played 旋律，曲调
resonator	/ˈrezəneɪtə/	n.	a piece of equipment that makes the sound of a musical instrument louder 共鸣器
intuition	/ˌɪntjuˈɪʃən/	n.	the ability to understand or know something because of a feeling rather than by considering the facts 直觉
pitch	/pɪtʃ/	n.	how high or low a note or other sound is 音调，音高
pestilence	/ˈpestɪləns/	n.	a disease that spreads quickly and kills a lot of people 瘟疫
Confucius	/kənˈfjuːʃəs/	n.	a Chinese philosopher whose ideas encouraged justice and peace, and who taught social and moral principles which had a great influence on Chinese society 孔子
ambience	/ˈæmbɪəns/	n.	the character of a place or the quality it seems to have 氛围，环境
somber	/ˈsɒmbə/	adj.	sad and serious 忧郁的，严峻的
prevail	/prɪˈveɪl/	vi.	to be common among a group of people or area at a particular time 盛行，流行
distressed	/dɪˈstrest/	adj.	very upset 忧愁的，苦恼的
languorous	/ˈlæŋgərəs/	adj.	lacking spirit or liveliness 倦怠的，无精打采的
long-drawn-out		adj.	continuing for a longer time than is wanted or necessary 冗长的，拖长了的
hearty	/ˈhɑːtɪ/	adj.	strong and healthy 健壮的
pious	/ˈpaɪəs/	adj.	strongly believing in religion, and living in a way which shows this belief 虔诚的
majestic	/məˈdʒestɪk/	adj.	very big, impressive, or beautiful 庄严的，雄伟壮丽的
lucid	/ˈluːsɪd/	adj.	expressed in a way that is clear and easy to understand 明晰的
affectionate	/əˈfekʃənɪt/	adj.	showing feelings of liking or love 亲切的

lewd	/luːd/	adj.	(of behaviour, speech, dress, etc.) sexual in an obvious and rude way 下流的
immoral	/ɪˈmɒrəl/	adj.	morally wrong 道德败坏的
degenerate	/dɪˈdʒenəreɪt/	vi.	to become worse than before in quality 衰退的，退化的
chaotic	/keɪˈɒtɪk/	adj.	in a state of chaos 混乱的
ritual	/ˈrɪtʃuəl/	n.	a ceremony that is always performed in the same way, in order to mark an important religious or social occasion 仪式，典礼
rueful	/ˈruːfəl/	adj.	feeling sorry and full of regret 悔恨的
restraint	/rɪsˈtreɪnt/	n.	calm sensible controlled behaviour, especially in a situation when it is difficult to stay calm 抑制
aspiration	/ˌæspəˈreɪʃən/	n.	a strong desire to have or achieve something 志向，抱负
sequence of chords			和弦模进
vibration	/vaɪˈbreɪʃən/	n.	a continuous slight shaking movement 震动
in tune with			harmonious with 与……协调
irritable	/ˈɪrɪtəbəl/	adj.	getting annoyed quickly or easily 急躁的，易怒的
out-of-sorts		adj.	feeling a little ill or upset 心绪烦乱
out of tune			not harmonious（与……)不协调
aligned	/əˈlaɪnd/	adj.	in line with 标准一致的
sensitivity	/ˌsensɪˈtɪvɪti/	n.	quality or degree of being sensitive 敏感性
discord	/ˈdɪskɔːd/	n.	disagreement or arguing between people 不和，纷争
isolate	/ˈaɪsəleɪt/	vt.	to separate one person, group, or thing from other people or things 使孤立，隔离
liberate	/ˈlɪbəreɪt/	vt.	to free someone from feelings or conditions that make their life unhappy or difficult 使解脱，使解放
jingle	/ˈdʒɪŋɡəl/	n.	a short song used in advertisements（广告中的）短曲，短歌
assail	/əˈseɪl/	vt.	to worry or upset 困扰
string quartets			a group of four stringed instruments (such as violin, cello, double bass, etc.) 弦乐四重奏
cassette tape			盒式磁带
Peer Gynt Suite			皮尔金组曲
lull	/lʌl/	vt.	to make someone feel calm or as if they want to sleep 使昏昏欲睡

Unit 4 Music

Notes:

Bach (1685–1750) was a German composer and organist. His works for solo instruments— the six sonatas and partitas for violin, the six cello suites (and the Partita for solo flute) may be listed among the most profound works in the repertoire. His best-known orchestral works are the Brandenburg concertos. In addition, he also wrote a number of cantatas.

Tchaikovsky (1840–1893) was a Russian composer of the Romantic era. Some of his best works are *The 1812 Overture, Swan Lake and Piano Concerto No.1*.

Brahms (1833–1897) was a German composer of the Romantic period. Some of his famous works are Hungarian Dance No. 5, and Wiegenlied, Op. 49 No. 4 which is universally known as Brahms' Lullaby.

Confucius (551BC–479BC) was a Chinese thinker and social philosopher, whose teachings and philosophy have deeply influenced Chinese, Korean, Japanese, and Vietnamese thought and life.

Pythagoras (born between 580 and 572 BC, died between 500 and 490 BC) was an Ionian Greek mathematician who is best known for the Pythagorean theorem. He is often revered as a great mathematician, mystic and scientist. Herodotus referred to him as "the most able philosopher among the Greeks".

Haydn (1732–1809) was an Austrian composer and one of the most prominent composers of the classical period, and is called by some the "Father of the Symphony". Some famous works are String Quartet in D minor, Symphony No.94 in G major "Surprise" and Symphony No.92 in G major "Oxford" No.92G.

Grieg (1843–1907) was a Norwegian composer and pianist who composed in the Romantic period. He is best known for his Piano Concerto in A minor, for his incidental music to Henrik Ibsen's play Peer Gynt, and for his collection of piano miniatures Lyric Pieces.

Reading Comprehension

I. Summarize the text into a few sentences, which indicate the main idea of the article.

_____

_____

II. Answer the following questions.

1. What is the power of music? What is the consequence if people ignore the power

of music?

2. How can music influence people's lives?

3. Why would the ancient Chinese emperors send wise men to visit villages and listen to the music being played?

4. Why did Pythagoras advise people to begin and end each day with music?

5. How do advertisers use music to persuade customers to buy their products? Can you use some examples to illustrate your points?

III. Judge, according to the text, whether the following statements are true or false. For false statements, write the facts in parentheses.

1. Although our responses to music may not go into conscious awareness, they still affect us subconsciously.
   (   )

2. Music is powerful mainly because much of our response to it occurs above the level of consciousness.
   (   )

3. Confucius believed that music had a great influence on the mental state and also the political and psychological ambience of a whole nation.
   (   )

4. We seldom think about what we listen to when we go to sleep in the evening, yet we think much about what we awaken to in the morning.
   (   )

5. People who are not "morning people" may feel a little too stimulated with Haydn string quartets.
   (   )

6. In ancient times, both Pythagoras and classroom teachers realized that music could change behavior.
   (   )

IV. Paraphrase the following sentences within the context.

1. (Para.1) Psychologist Roberto Assagioli, author of *Psychosynthesis*, believes music can facilitate the development of our highest potential as human beings

or it can plunge us into despair and depression and even cause disease.

2. (Para. 2) We are usually not aware that our pulse speeds up with the rhythm of a certain piece of music, or that a certain melodic pattern may trigger the memory of an open field we used to play in as children.

3. (Para. 5) Unconsciously, the right music creates an affinity with the product that we would not consciously choose.

4. (Para. 9) He believed in a cosmic vibration that could enter the being through the mind. One in tune with this cosmic vibration was a healthy person.

5. (Para. 10) When we feel irritable or out-of-sorts, we are likely to be out of tune with this cosmic vibration. When things feel just right, there is a deep knowing that we are aligned to it.

6. (Para. 12) News of world disasters, hard rock, endless commercial jingles assails our ears.

Vocabulary Exercises

I. **Fill in each blank with one of the following words from each pair and note the difference of meaning between them. Change the form when necessary.**
   1. SOMBER   SOBER
      a. Some black coffee may _____ her up.
      b. The expert gave a _____ assessment of the situation.

c. After mother's funeral, we were all in a _____ mood.
d. He is a nice and hardworking guy when he is _____.
e. His expression was _____ as he listened to the report of the accident.

2. ASPIRATION   INSPIRATION

a. She was filled with a high level of political _____.
b. Walking around the lake, he had a sudden flash of _____.
c. Don't you have any hope or _____ for your future?
d. Many poets and artists have drawn their _____ from nature.

3. AWAKEN   WAKE

a. He was _____ by a loud bang at two in the morning.
b. When she _____ in the hotel the next day, the sun was streaming through the windows.
c. We must _____ people to the seriousness of the situation.
d. It's time you _____ up to the fact that it's a tough world.

II. Fill in the blank in each sentence with a word or phrase taken from the box in its appropriate form.

| resonator | frazzle | affinity | soothing | sputtering |
| manipulate | pestilence | therapeutic | languorous | degenerate |

1. A _____ was raging in the flood-stricken area.
2. Lying on the beach, he was filled with an agreeable _____.
3. A clever politician knows how to _____ public opinion in his favor.
4. The whole street kept _____ with laughter and music on Christmas Eve.
5. Walking along the mountain road for a whole day, I was worn to a _____.
6. Lucy made a cup of tea to _____ her nerves.
7. The dispute _____ into a complete brawl.
8. This book tells us how one woman turned her remarkable _____ for animals into a full-time career.
9. Some people claim that the herb has _____ value for treating pain.
10. All of a sudden, the fire _____ and died.

Unit 4 Music

Translation Exercises

Translate each of the following sentences into English, using the word or phrase given in the brackets.

1. 在校学生可以参加各种各样的校园活动。对他们而言,大学是全面发展自身潜力的理想场所。(plunge into)

2. 地方政府向卫生部汇报了正在蔓延的禽流感疫情后,卫生部立刻对此做出反应。(response)

3. 失业后,简陋的住房和微薄的收入加快了他家庭的破裂。(speed up)

4. 学生就业压力大、心理承受能力差以及价值观的偏离已成为当代大学生心理健康问题高发的原因。(arise from)

5. 在古希腊和古罗马对外扩张的过程中,他们的文化也渗透到许多西方国家,影响了西方文化的发展。(penetrate into)

6. 当我落下,又被弹起时,感觉自己像一只在空中自由飞翔的云雀。(feel like)

7. 由于缺少灭火器,五十多人在这场火灾中丧生,这使我们意识到需要采取更多的安全防范措施。(wake up to)

8. 我们不能用老一套的教育方法来教导现在的孩子,因为这些方法已经与时代不合拍了。(attune to)

Text II

Sport and Music

> **Pre-reading Questions**
>
> 1. What is the Olympic anthem? On which occasion can you hear it most often?
> 2. Is there a close connection between sports and music? What Olympic events are accompanied by music? If music is turned off, will the competitions achieve the same excellence as otherwise?

1 *Only out of an intimate union of seriousness and playfulness can true art arise. (Goethe)*

2 From earliest times, sport and music, two highly individual and autonomous partners, have formed a fragile and at times intense sporadic union. Pierre de Coubertin, an enthusiastic amateur of music and admirer of Wagner, dreamed in vain of having a great master compose a grand symphony on sport. His hope that the music section of the Olympic art competitions would produce something other than ephemeral circumstantial pieces with sporty sounding titles also remained unfulfilled.

3 Nevertheless, the ties between the two fields are close, and far transcend the realm of modern sports events which use a musical accompaniment. They are based on many common characteristics, although these often diverge at different levels.

4 Sport and music coincide discernibly or audibly in four aspects:
- in play and movement, which follow set rules but can be varied almost inexhaustibly in constantly new and surprising ways;
- in continuous mental and physical training for discipline and excellence that forge the way toward achieving a virtuoso performance. This standard can only be maintained through a constant testing of skills against those of the competitors;
- in the performance pyramid, where millions of amateurs form the base while the elite virtuosos make up the "international league";

- and in the virtually universal language which these two cultural spheres constitute as forms of expression.

5   Movement is the common denominator between forms of expression in sport and music, as clearly reflected in the English and French use of the word (mouvement in French) to designate sections of musical works such as symphonies or sonatas. It is revealing that Isaac Stern uses sports metaphors to describe the challenges of performance: "Every single performance absolutely has to have something spontaneous about it. The essence of making music is constant rediscovery. It is as if your head was filled only with music, with musical ideas and a physical sense of the start and the finish, of what you are about to begin and for which you have to prepare, like an athlete preparing to make a jump or a throw, or whatever. Before anything actually happens, for a fraction of a second you concentrate on achieving exactly what you have prepared for; your thoughts merge together and you can see, feel and hear how they will come out—and, hopefully, the audience will enjoy it."

6   In addition to these parallels, in which mental effort and physical execution are said to act in unison, there are differences, divergences and dividing factors. These complex factors are clearly illustrated by the relationship between music and sport which one sees in choreographed movements that are accompanied and stimulated by music. In figure skating, this unison has been elevated in French with a lofty reference to "art" (patinage artistique). Rhythmic gymnastics, synchronized swimming and dressage are performed "on the waves of music", which may be composed for the occasion or borrowed from the works of great composers or from popular music. It is in dressage that we find the first specifically sports-related compositions: the Balleto cavallo by the Vienna court composer Johann Heinrich Schmelzer von Ehrenruef, which was revived and put to practical use by Gabriella Grillo, Olympic dressage champion with the German team in 1976, was written in 1667.

7   The relationship between sport and music has a number of oddities. Perhaps the most original configuration—called Match for three players—was created by Mauricio Kagel after a dream. This composition, which Kagel even produced himself for television, constitutes a tonal duel between two cellos with the percussion playing the role of referee. This "instrumental theatre", with its predetermined gestures and patterns, is inspired by something that modern sport often lacks, namely a sense of irony.

8   Any list of the great composers who have produced minor but high-calibre sports-inspired works would not be complete without Leonard Bernstein, Benjamin Britten, Leos Janacek, Bohuslav Martinu, and Alexandre Tcherepnin.

9   Although the Olympic Games have not been influenced by the "dogma of Wagnerian aesthetics", it was Coubertin's idea that they should always be closely associated with music and sometimes even venture courageously beyond the ordinary, for example by using electronic sounds in the opening of the X Olympic Winter Games in Grenoble in 1968. The ballet-like union of dance movement and music characterizes the performances at Opening Ceremonies, which are a form of cultural self-representation.

10   After his Olympisches Reigen of 1936, Carl Orff wrote a more intimate type of music on the theme of a medieval song for the Games in 1972. In Munich, the traditional pathos of the march music for the participants' opening parade gave way to the sounds of a more folkloric type of music, alluding to the guest countries and played by a big band. In 1936, incidentally, one of Coubertin's dearest wishes was fulfilled: in Berlin, Beethoven's Ninth Symphony was played, with Schiller's Ode to Joy, which is now the European anthem.

11   The question of the musical logo, i.e. the melody which is identified with the Olympic Games or other championships, is particularly vexatious. The prerequisites for these signature tunes—a striking form of expression, brevity and "catchiness"—force composers to resort to stereotypes with ringing trumpets and heavy drums. This circumstantial music only rarely outlives the occasion in question. It was an inspired idea for UEFA to go back to a reliable source like Händel to find the signature tune for television broadcasts of its champions' league.

12   Thanks to television as a universal media presence, musical hits play a quasi-missionary role at international events. Not a single symphony orchestra in the world could have guaranteed Ravel's Bolero the popularity it acquired through the skating performance of ice-dancers Torvill and Dean. And the musical event that marked the 1990 football world championships, a concert given in the Caracalla baths in Rome by the tenor "dream team" Carreras, Domingo and Pavarotti, gave millions access to world-class belcanto and led to repeat performances by the trio, who, like pop groups, performed in huge stadia to enthusiastic audiences. Purists may turn up their noses at this aspect of the relationship between sport and music. However, the communicative synergy

attained by these two partners remains unchallenged, and it draws music beyond the narrow confines of the elite and the connoisseurs.

13   The title "Olympia" or "Olympiad" occurs surprisingly often in lists of musical works. However, they are mostly operas of the Italian or French baroque period. The librettos, by authors such as Voltaire or Metastasio, present various scenes from Greek mythology. Unfortunately, the modern Olympic world has so far failed to find an adequate musical representation. One can only speculate as to why this should be.

14   With the exception of the accompanying cultural programme, music understandably plays a supporting role at the Olympic Games. This observation is not intended to detract in any way from the efforts to give this international event an appropriate tonal framework, for here too, the highest quality is called for. The Olympic Games set composers this challenge again and again. Will they ever find the perfect work? Such an idealistic hope seems unrealistic. And yet Goethe's words about true art, which can arise only out of an intimate union of seriousness and playfulness, could become a refrain for the next Olympic century.

(1,217 words)

Reading Comprehension

I. **Answer the following questions with the information you read from the passage.**
   1. What was the hope of Pierre de Coubertin as an enthusiastic amateur of music and admirer of Wagner?
   2. What common characteristics do sport and music share?
   3. What sports metaphors did Isaac Stern use to describe the challenges of performance?
   4. How do mental effort and physical execution act in unison? Explain with examples.
   5. Make a list of the composers mentioned in this passage and their contributions to sport.

II. Topics for discussion and reflection.

1. Enjoy the Olympic theme songs in history and discuss with your partners about their distinct features.
2. Sport is entertainment, so is music, especially in its lighter forms. Discuss how they interact with each other by illustrating some sports music, such as Hubert Bath's march *Out of the Blue* for Sports Report and Puccini's *Nessun Dorma* and Fauré's *Pavane* for the World Cup, etc.

Exercises for Integrated Skills

I. Dictation

Listen to the following passage. Altogether the passage will be read to you four times. During the first reading, which will be read at normal speed, listen and try to understand the meaning. For the second and third readings, the passage will be read sentence by sentence, or phrase by phrase, with intervals of 15 to 20 seconds. The last reading will be done at normal speed again and during this time you should check your work. You will then be given 2 minutes to check through your work once more.

II. Cloze

Fill in each blank in the passage below with a word or phrase taken from the box in its appropriate form.

prolong	equal	poison	premature	addict
medicine	brainwash	virtual	negative	classical
detriment	metabolic	low	converse	process
hemisphere	awe	wild	conscious	move

Unit 4 Music

Music can ___1___ the soul. It can be a very strong influence. Some music can calm us down; some music can make us ___2___ ! How does music affect us?

Music is used in a variety of ways. It is used in the ___3___ field as a source of research and as a sort of therapy as well. Music has been used as therapy for seizures, to ___4___ blood pressure, treat ADD (Attention Deficit Disorder) children, treat mental illness, treat depression, aid in healing, and treat stress and insomnia and ___5___ infants.

Musicologist Julius Portnoy found that music can change ___6___ rates, increase or decrease blood pressure, affect energy levels and digestion, positively or ___7___ , depending on the type of music. Calming music, such as ___8___ music was found to have a very calming effect on the body, and cause the increase of endorphins, thirty minutes of such music was ___9___ to the effect of a dose of valium. Both ___10___ of the brain are involved in ___11___ music. The music in these studies is not the "lyrics", but the music itself, the melody, the tones, the tunes, the rhythm and the chords.

___12___ , music has also been documented to cause sickness. The right, or wrong music, rather, can be like a ___13___ to the body. Studies have been done on plants that loud hard rock music, for instance, killed plants and soft classical music made the plants grow faster. Music is very powerful, like a drug and can even be an ___14___ . In the case of Patty Hearst, it was documented that music was used in aid of ___15___ her. In the book, *Elevator Music*, by Joseph Lanza, it states that certain types of music, over ___16___ periods in certain conditions, were shown to cause seizures.

In the book, *The Secret Power of Music*, by David Tame, it says, "music is more than a language; it is the language of languages. It can be said that of all the arts, there is none other that more powerfully moves and changes the ___17___ ."

It can be said that music is a very powerful and ___18___ tool that can have positive effects, ___19___ life saving mentally and physically when used in the right context, but has equally destructive and ___20___ potential if used negatively.

Oral Activities

Activity One: The Power of Music

Each student prepares for a 2-minute speech about his/her favorite song/music/singer/ composer and present it before the class.

Activity Two: Role Play—Mozart Effect

The Mozart Effect suggests that "listening to Mozart makes you smarter", or that early childhood exposure to classical music has a beneficial effect on mental development.

Prepare a role-play based on the following situation: suppose you are a senior high school student and will take the college entrance examination in a month. You believe in the Mozart Effect and like to listen to music even when doing homework, but your parents are strongly against it.

2 students will play the roles of your parents. You are going to persuade your parents into accepting your idea that music can help you better study for the crucial exam.

Writing Practice

Note Writing: A Note of Thanks

In the "Global Harmony" Concert Series during the Olympics, three world-famous Sopranos, Angela Gheorghiu, Renee Fleming, and Cao Xiumei are due to perform in Beijing. Your friend, Mike, knows that you are a music fan and offers you a ticket. Write a thank-you note to Mike, expressing your excitement and extending your gratitude.

3 April, 20 _____

Dear Mike,

Sincerely,
John

Composition Writing

Are you familiar with the theme songs played at the Olympic opening ceremonies? *Reachout* by John Williams in the 1984 Olympics, *Hand in Hand* by Koreana in 1988, *The Flame* by Tina Arena in 2000, and *You and Me* by Liu Huan and Sarah Brightman in 2008. Write a composition about your favorite Olympic theme song in about 120 words. The reasons why you like it should be included in the composition.

Unit 5 Disasters

Warm-up Activities

1. List as many natural disasters as you know. Which one do you think causes the most serious damage?
2. Complete the following crossword puzzle about different types of disasters.

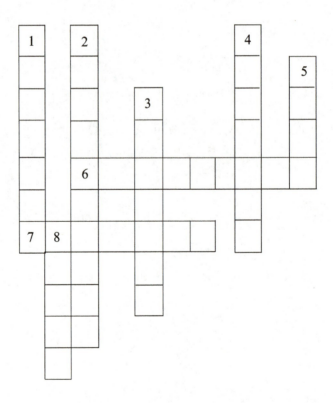

Unit 5 Disasters

Across

6. a powerful, swirling storm that begins over a warm sea
7. a Japanese word with the English translation, "harbor wave"

Down

1. a period of hot, dry weather with too little rain
2. a sudden shaking of the earth's surface
3. an extremely violent storm consisting of air that spins very quickly
4. a mountain with a large hole at the top, through which very hot liquid rock is sometimes forced out
5. hot flames that destroy things
8. a period of very bad weather when there is a lot of rain or snow, strong winds

Text I

We Are the Problem

> *Pre-reading Questions*
> 1. Are natural disasters closely related to environmental destruction? Give an example to support your opinion.
> 2. Should people move to safer ground if they live in a place frequently hit by natural disasters?

1   A hazard exists where a natural event is likely to harm people or property. Similarly, a disaster is a hazardous event that affects humans or property. A major natural event—an earthquake, a volcanic eruption, a landslide, a flood, or a hurricane or a tornado—in a remote area is merely a part of the ongoing process of nature. Problems arise when people place themselves in environments where they can be impacted by such major events. It makes no sense to blame nature for natural events that have been going on for hundreds or millions of

years. The problem is not the natural event, but humans.

2 The solution then would seem simple. Keep people from locations that are hazardous. Unfortunately, that is easier said than done. Nomadic cultures learned to go with the flow; they learned to live with nature rather than fight it. Impacted by major events, they merely moved to safer ground, leaving a floodplain when the water began to rise, or moving away from a volcano when it began to rumble.

3 Part of the problem now is that there are billions of us humans. As civilization evolved, we moved to where we could live comfortably and where we had the resources to meet our needs for food, water, energy, shelter, and transportation. We settled along coastlines and rivers where water was available, crops would grow, the climate was hospitable, and we could trade goods with other groups of people. We settled near volcanoes where the soil was fertile for crops. As time went on, we concentrated in groups for defensive reasons; towns grew larger but essentially in the same locations that were most suitable for our basic needs.

4 As our cities grew, our infrastructure became entrenched. Our shelters, our transportation systems, and our communication networks became permanent—houses, stores, factories, roads, bridges, dams, water supply systems, and power lines. When natural events impacted us, we fought back. We built levees to hold back rising rivers, not realizing that with our towns built on floodplains, we were living in the natural high-water paths of many rivers. We should not have built in these places to begin with, but back then we did not know any better. We should have built our towns on higher terraces above the level of floods. We could have still used floodplains to grow crops but abandon them temporarily whenever the water rose. Unfortunately, that is all in hindsight. Our towns grew up where they did, and we have to live with the consequences.

5 We continue to make poor choices. As the people of industrialized countries became more affluent and as free time and efficient transportation became widely available, we began making choices based on leisure, recreation, and aesthetics. We began building homes close to streams, on the edges of sea cliffs,

on offshore barrier islands, in the "shelter" and view of spectacular cliffs and majestic volcanoes. When the larger natural events come along, we complain that nature is out of control. But nature is not the problem: we are the problem. We should live in safer places.

6   People take risks all the time. Most people understand that there are risks in all aspects of life; we accept many of them through lack of choice. There is little we can do about a stray meteorite unexpectedly nailing us, and we know that the odds of it happening are remote. Walking in the forest, we know that trees sometimes fall; we know the odds of one hitting us are remote so we do not think about it. Every time we get in a car and head out on the road, we understand that some other drivers may cause a collision by being drunk, by falling asleep, by running a red light, or by merely being inattentive. Yet we accept the risks because, although accidents happen, we feel it is not likely to happen to us.

7   The same feelings cloud our judgment when we decide to build or buy a house in a location that suits our fancy. That spectacular view over the ocean, that place on a beautiful sandy beach, that tranquil site at the edge of a scenic stream—these are all desirable places to live. Those attractive locations are also subject to natural hazards that endanger our houses and perhaps also our lives.

8   Even people who are knowledgeable of particular natural hazards sometimes succumb to the lure of a great place. Yes, catastrophes have happened to others, "but it won't happen to me." Our wanting "something special" clouds our judgment. There are those who are well aware of a particular hazard but are willing to live with the consequences, both physical and financial. In an area prone to earthquakes, they incur the expense of building earthquake-resistant homes and purchasing expensive earthquake insurance. In a landslide-prone area, they install expensive drainage systems and may even pay for rock bolting the bedrock under their houses. Because landslide insurance is not generally available, they are willing to risk losing the complete value of their houses. For most of us, however, our home is the largest investment we will ever make; we borrow heavily, paying for it over fifteen to thirty years. Unfortunately, if the house is destroyed in a landslide, we are still liable for paying off the mortgage, even though the house no longer exists.

9   Though no one can control the forces of nature or predict the destruction of the next major event, people do have choices to minimize the risk. But as people

continue to be naive thinking "It won't happen to me", when a natural disaster hits their home, they have only themselves to blame.

(950 words)

Words and Expressions

hazard	/ˈhæzəd/	n.	something that may be dangerous, or cause accidents or problems 危险, 隐患
property	/ˈprɒpətɪ/	n.	the thing or things that someone owns 财产
hazardous	/ˈhæzədəs/	adj.	dangerous, especially to people's health or safety 有害的
volcanic eruption			火山喷发
landslide	/ˈlændslaɪd/	n.	a sudden fall of a lot of earth or rocks down a hill, cliff, etc. 山崩, 滑坡
tornado	/tɔːˈneɪdəʊ/	n.	an extremely violent storm consisting of air that spins very quickly and causes a lot of damage 龙卷风
ongoing	/ˈɒnˌɡəʊɪŋ/	adj.	continuing, or continuing to develop 不断发展中的
impact	/ˈɪmpækt/	vi.&vt.	to have an important or noticeable effect on someone or something 产生(重要或明显的)影响
make sense			to be reasonable 合乎情理, 有道理
nomadic culture			游牧文化
floodplain	/ˈflʌdpleɪn/	n.	the large area of flat land on either side of a river that is sometimes covered with water 洪泛区
rumble	/ˈrʌmbəl/	vi.	to make a continuous low sound 发出隆隆声
coastline	/ˈkəʊstlaɪn/	n.	the land on the edge of the coast, especially the shape of the land as seen from the air 海岸线
hospitable	/ˈhɒspɪtəbəl/	adj.	providing good conditions for living or growing 适宜的, 有利的
fertile	/ˈfɜːtaɪl/	adj.	bearing, producing, or capable of producing vegetation abundantly 肥沃的
essentially	/ɪˈsenʃəlɪ/	adv.	relating to the most important characteristics or ideas of something 本质上, 根本上

Unit 5 Disasters

infrastructure	/ˈɪnfrəˌstrʌktʃə/	n.	the basic systems and structures that a country or organization needs in order to work properly 基础设施,基础结构
entrenched	/ɪnˈtrentʃt/	adj.	strongly established and not likely to change 牢固确立的
power line			输电线
levee	/ˈlevɪ/	n.	a special wall built to stop a river from flooding 防洪堤
terrace	/ˈterəs/	n.	a flat raised area 平台
hindsight	/ˈhaɪndsaɪt/	n.	the ability to understand a situation only after it has happened 后见之明,事后聪明
affluent	/ˈæfluənt/	adj.	having plenty of money, nice houses, expensive things, etc. 富裕的,富足的
aesthetics	/iːsˈθetɪks/	n.	the study of beauty, especially beauty in art (审)美学
cliff	/klɪf/	n.	a large area of rock or a mountain with a very steep side, often on the edge of the sea or a river 悬崖
offshore	/ˈɒfʃɔː/	adj.	in the ocean, away from the shore 靠近海岸的
spectacular	/spekˈtækjʊlə/	adj.	very impressive 壮观的,精彩的
stray	/streɪ/	adj.	accidentally separated from other things of the same kind 零落的
meteorite	/ˈmiːtɪəraɪt/	n.	a piece of rock or metal from space that has landed on earth 陨石
nail	/neɪl/	vt.	to catch someone 抓住(某人)
odds	/ɒdz; ɑːdz/	n.	likelihood of something that will or will not happen 可能性
cloud	/klaʊd/	vt.	to confuse or impair 把……搞糊涂
tranquil	/ˈtræŋkwɪl/	adj.	pleasantly calm, quiet, and peaceful 宁静的
scenic	/ˈsiːnɪk/	adj.	surrounded by views of beautiful countryside 景色优美的
desirable	/dɪˈzaɪərəbəl/	adj.	worth having and wanted by most people 值得拥有的
be subject to			易受(尤指坏事)影响的
endanger	/ɪnˈdeɪndʒə/	vt.	to put someone or something in a dangerous situation 危及
succumb	/səˈkʌm/	vi.	to lose the determination to oppose something 屈服

lure	/lʊə, ljʊə/	n.	something that attracts people, or the quality of being able to do this 诱惑力
prone	/prəʊn/	adj.	likely to do something or suffer from something, especially something bad or harmful 很可能……的
incur	/ɪnˈkɜː/	vt.	to experience something, usually something unpleasant, as a result of actions you have taken 遭受, 招致
earthquake-resistant	/ˈɜːθkweɪk ˌrɪˈzɪstənt/	adj.	抗震的
install	/ɪnˈstɔːl/	vt.	to put a piece of equipment somewhere and connect it so that it is ready to be used 安装
drainage system			排水系统
bolt	/bəʊlt/	vt.	to fasten two things together using a bolt 用螺栓固定住
bedrock	/ˈbedrɒk/	n.	solid rock in the ground below the soil or sand 基岩
investment	/ɪnˈvestmənt/	n.	something that you buy or do because it will be useful later 投资, 投入
liable	/ˈlaɪəbəl/	adj.	legally responsible for the cost of something 有……责任的
mortgage	/ˈmɔːgɪdʒ/	n.	legal arrangement by which you borrow money from a bank or similar organization in order to buy a house, and pay back the money over a period of time 抵押借款, 按揭

Reading Comprehension

I. Match the items in Column A with the items in Column B.

Column A

A. Earthquake

B. Landslide

Column B

A. the slipping down of a mass of rocks or earth on a steep slope

B. a great flow of water over the land

C. Flood
D. Hurricane
E. Tsunami

C. a tropical cyclone with winds that are usually accompanied by rain, thunder, and lightning
D. a tidal wave caused by an underwater earthquake or volcanic eruption
E. a shaking or trembling of a portion of the earth

II. **Answer the following questions.**
1. What does "disaster" mean? How does the problem of natural disasters lie in humans and not in the event itself?
2. What did nomads learn to deal with the hazards?
3. Where did people prefer to live with the development of civilization?
4. As towns and cities grew up, what did people do to combat the natural events that impacted their safety?
5. How do most people feel about the risks in life? What is your own attitude towards the risks in daily life?

III. **Judge, according to the text, whether the following statements are true or false. For false statements, write the facts in parentheses.**
1. It makes sense to rebuke nature for natural disasters that have been going on for many years.
   (   )
2. As civilization evolved, people settled near volcanoes where the soil was fertile for crops.
   (   )
3. People could have still used floodplains to grow crops but abandon them permanently whenever the water rose.
   (   )
4. There are many measures we can take to escape from a stray meteorite unexpectedly nailing us.
   (   )
5. People accept risks because they feel it is almost impossible to happen to them.
   (   )

IV. **Paraphrase the following sentences within the context.**
1. (Para. 3) As time went on, we concentrated in groups for defensive reasons;

towns grew larger but essentially in the same locations that were most suitable for our basic needs.

2. (Para. 5) As the people of industrialized countries became more affluent and as free time and efficient transportation became widely available, we began making choices based on leisure, recreation, and aesthetics.

3. (Para. 6) There is little we can do about a stray meteorite unexpectedly nailing us, and we know that the odds of it happening are remote.

4. (Para. 7) The same feelings cloud our judgment when we decide to build or buy a house in a location that suits our fancy.

5. (Para. 7) Those attractive locations are also subject to natural hazards that endanger our houses and perhaps also our lives.

6. (Para. 8) In an area prone to earthquakes, they incur the expense of building earthquake-resistant homes and purchasing expensive earthquake insurance.

Vocabulary Exercises

I. **Fill in each blank with one of the following words from each pair and note the difference of meaning between them. Change the form when necessary.**
   1. EVOLVE   REVOLVE
      a. The company has _____ over the years into a multi-million dollar organization.

Unit 5 Disasters

   b. The earth _____ both around the sun and on its own axis.
   c. Ever since they had children, their conversations and arguments were always _____ around childcare problems.
   d. Some animals have _____ camouflage to protect themselves from predators.
   e. The restaurant slowly _____, giving amazing views of the town.

2. **INCUR   OCCUR**
   a. If any of these symptoms _____ after you take the medicine, consult your doctor immediately.
   b. The movie has _____ the wrath of both audiences and critics.
   c. Earthquake is a common _____ in these areas of the country.
   d. Please detail any expenses you _____ while attending conference.
   e. It never _____ to her that she might be falling in love with him.

II. **Fill in the blank in each sentence with a word or phrase taken from the box. Change the form where necessary.**

> spectacular   make no sense   rumble   hold back   hindsight
> entrench   be prone to   be subject to   aesthetics   succumb
> infrastructure   affluent

1. The war has badly damaged the country's physical _____.
2. With the wisdom of _____, I should have taken your advice.
3. It's very difficult to change beliefs that have become so deeply _____ over the years.
4. As far as I know, she was _____ depressions even as a teenager.
5. It would only be a matter of time before he _____ to our company's temptation.
6. We could hear trains _____ past the town.
7. It _____ to find the root causes of the trouble.
8. These sandbags will _____ the flood waters for a while.
9. You can enjoy the _____ scenery of the mountainous area from the helicopter.

10. People in this region are living in _____.
11. In recent years, she has been _____ to heart attacks.
12. I like furniture to be both functional and _____ pleasing.

III. Choose a word or phrase that best completes each of the following sentences.

1. Watching me pulling the calf awkwardly to the barn, the Irish milkmaid fought hard to _____ her laughter.
   A. hold back   B. hold on   C. hold out   D. hold up
2. We should manage to _____ all our debts within three years.
   A. pay for   B. pay out   C. pay over   D. pay off
3. The concert was brilliant, it certainly lived _____ all my expectations.
   A. with   B. up to   C. out   D. by
4. Weight lifting, or any other sport that builds up your muscles, can make bones become denser and less _____ to injury.
   A. attached   B. immune   C. prone   D. reconciled
5. In _____ of what you have said, I think we should reconsider the proposal.
   A. opinion   B. sight   C. view   D. perspective

Translation Exercises

Translate each of the following sentences into English, using the word or phrase given in the brackets.

1. 这件大衣的布料和款式都很好又很便宜,你何必非买那件贵的呢？
   (make sense)

2. 经历了大自然的一次次报复之后,人们已经达成共识:人类只有与大自然和谐共存才能求得自身的繁衍和发展。(go with)

3. 一排排白杨树阻挡着沙漠的延伸,但沙尘总会时不时借着强劲的风力,一口吞没这里的庄稼。(hold back)

4. 台风到来时,我们要尽可能待在屋里,尽量不要外出行走,更不要去台风经过的地区游玩。(come along)

Unit 5   Disasters

5. 创新也是需要冒险的,因为你不知道新项目的成果是否会得到认可。
(take risk)

6. 这个地区常遭破坏性季风的袭击,严重时许多民房都被夷为平地,因此那儿的居民一直是政府优抚的对象。(be subject to)

7. 在市场经济的大潮中,有些政府官员抵挡不住金钱的诱惑,最终走上了犯罪的道路。(succumb to)

8. 好的雇主不仅仅是对员工负责,同时也要担负起对股东和社会应承担的责任。(be liable for)

Text II

After the Tornado

Pre-reading Questions

1. How much do you know about tornadoes? What do you know about similar storms?
2. As a proverb goes, "Calamity is Man's true touchstone." Draw from your personal experiences to testify the proverb.

1   Except for the dreary, overcast weather, last November 15 was an ordinary midweek morning in Montgomery, Alabama. Thirty-one children were doing their usual things at the Learning Zone Day Care Center: the babies were napping, the toddlers were playing. The older kids, ages three to five, were at the indoor playground on the opposite side of the Fun Zone, the 60,000-square-foot entertainment complex that leased space to the child-care facility. On evenings and weekends, the Fun Zone was always packed. People came to roller-skate, ride bumper cars, climb the rock wall, and play arcade games. That day, all was quiet but for the shouts of preschoolers bouncing in the ball pit and crawling

through the jungle gym maze in what workers called the soft play area.

2   Liberty Duke, director of the Learning Zone, was busy doing paperwork when sirens went off at about 10 a.m.. She didn't panic. Severe weather alerts are frequent  that time of year and usually signal a hard, drenching rain. Figuring the pots of mums in the entryway could use a good watering, she picked them up and took them outside.

3   Then the power went out. As Duke stood in the dark, she heard glass shatter. Gusts of wind blasted through the broken windows, sending ceiling tiles spinning through the air. She tried to open the door, but it barely budged. Peeking out a crack, she was shocked. The Fun Zone was gone. "All you could see was the sky," she says.

4   Across the parking lot, Lewis Harrison had just pulled into Car Audio Plus. He needed a new front speaker in his Chevy Blazer. Looking up, he and his buddy Bill Marcum saw a car hurtle over the roof of the post office. All of a sudden, they were in the middle of a raging tornado.

5   Stereo installer JJ Justiss ran to grab some equipment that had blown out of the shop. Behind him he saw the Fun Zone collapse into a mountain of metal and smoke. Grabbing his cell phone, he called 911 and took off, running so fast his Birkenstocks fell off in the driving rain.

6   Harrison had been to the Fun Zone many times with his six-year-old twin girls. He knew all about the kids in the day-care center. Everyone in the area did. He and Marcum ran toward the wreckage. Workers from Worth Cleaners, a few doors away, were right behind them.

7   By the time they arrived, Liberty Duke had made her way through the debris. Her four-year-old son, Justice, was one of the kids trapped inside. The silence was terrifying, Duke recalls. "We couldn't hear any crying. That was the scariest part."

8   She pointed the men toward what had been the soft play area. The 30-foot wall that had enclosed it was now a pile of cinder blocks. Justiss, a small, wiry

man, squirmed through the tangled tunnels of the jungle gym maze. "Hello!" he bellowed. "Anybody there?" He could hear gas hissing and power lines zapping overhead.

9   Harrison and Marcum tried another way in, climbing under and over fallen steel beams, looking for survivors. Fiberglass insulation burned their eyes, and concrete dust filled their lungs. Then, in the midst of it all, came a sound that seemed almost miraculous: children crying.

10 Pressing forward, the men picked through mounds of crushed cinder blocks. After three or four minutes of frantic digging, they uncovered the ball pit, which was encased in sturdy netting. There were the little ones, huddled together, barefoot and terrified, all screaming.

11 When the walls started to crumble, teachers Lekithia McQueen and Vonnmetria Hamilton had shielded the children with their own bodies. Strong winds blew McQueen's legs straight up in the air, and something sharp ripped her hand open, but she'd held on. She knew if she let go, her students would be sucked into the storm.

12 Pulling out his pocketknife, Justiss cut through the netting. "They were these itty-bitty kids," he says, "scared to death and wanting Mama. I would have been the same way."

13 He and Harrison jumped into the pit and started handing kids up over the wreckage, to the outstretched arms of Bill Marcum and Liberty Duke. Behind them, the dry cleaner employees fanned out to form a human chain. One by one, they handed the traumatized boys and girls down the line, until all were safely inside the cleaners.

14 The first girl Harrison reached bore an uncanny resemblance to his daughter Megan, which increased his intensity. Duke was nearly overcome with relief at the sight of the children—including her son. "They were covered with dust. It was the most beautiful thing I'd ever seen."

15 Inside, workers covered them with blankets that had been laundered for customers. Several people from New2u, a consignment boutique in the same shopping plaza, brought coats and sweaters for the kids, who were soaked from the rain and shivering.

16 Meanwhile, the men kept digging. When emergency vehicles arrived, all the children were safely accounted for. In the day-care center, everyone was unharmed as well.

17 　　"Total strangers saved the day," says Duke, whose son was one of two kids requiring medical attention, with a gash on his head that took 14 stitches. "He was crying, saying his school was broken before he learned to read. I told him that thanks to people we'd never met, he would learn to read at another school."

(891 words)

Reading Comprehension

I. Answer the following questions with the information you read from the passage.

1. What were the children doing at the Learning Zone Day Care Center before the tornado sirens wailed?
2. How did people react when the tornado headed down to Montgomery, Alabama?
3. What was the scariest part when the search and rescue work started?
4. Where did children get trapped? And what was the children's reaction?

II. Topics for discussion and reflection.

1. Do you think man can really defeat nature? What is the relationship between man and nature?
2. It is said that, "There is no love in disaster, but we have love in human's heart." How is it embodied in disasters?

Exercises for Integrated Skills

I. Dictation

　　Listen to the following passage. Altogether the passage will be read to you four times. During the first reading, which will be read at normal speed, listen and try to understand the meaning. For the second and third readings, the passage will be read sentence by sentence, or phrase by phrase, with intervals of 15 to 20 seconds. The last reading will be done at normal speed again and during this time you should check your work. You will then be given 2 minutes to check through your work once more.

Unit 5 Disasters

II. Cloze

Fill in each blank in the passage below with a word or phrase taken from the box in its appropriate form.

replace	interfere	persistent	moisture	duration
disaster	emergent	affect	whereas	zone
monitor	precipitation	serious	settle	developed
significant	usual	relief	normal	reliable

Drought is a period or condition of ___1___ dry weather within a geographic area where rainfall is normally present. During a drought there is a lack of ___2___. Droughts occur in all climatic ___3___. However, its characteristics vary ___4___ from one region to another.

Drought usually results in a water shortage that seriously ___5___ with human activity. Water-supply reservoirs empty, wells dry up, and crop damage ensues. Its ___6___ depends on the degree of the water shortage, size of area affected, and the ___7___ and warmth of the dry period. In many ___8___ countries, such as India, people place a great demand on water supply. During a drought when there is a lack of water, many of the poor die.

Most precipitation depends on water vapor carried by winds from an ocean or other sources of ___9___. If these moisture-carrying winds are ___10___ by winds from a dry region, or if they are modified by a downward motion, as in the center of an anticyclone, the weather is ___11___ dry and often ___12___ cloudless. If the drought period is short, it is known as a dry spell. A dry spell is usually more than 14 days without precipitation, ___13___ a severe drought may last for years.

Statistics indicate that every 22 years a major drought occurs in the United

States, most seriously ____14____ the Midwestern states. The drought of 1933–35, during which large areas of the Great Plains became known as the Dust Bowl, is an example of a ____15____ drought that took place in the United Sates. The effect of the drought was brought about by overcropping, overpopulation, and lack of ____16____ measures.

Although drought cannot be ____17____ predicted, certain precautions can be taken in drought-risk areas. These include construction of reservoirs to hold ____18____ water supplies, education to avoid overcropping and overgrazing, and programs to limit ____19____ in drought-prone areas. The Southern Africa Development Community ____20____ the crop and food situation in the region and alerts the people during periods of crisis.

Oral Activities

Activity One: When disaster strikes.

1. Describe the damages that a disaster would bring to a family, a city, or a country.
2. Tell a story related to a disaster, focusing on the courage or love that people displayed when they confronted misfortunes. It may be your personal experience or one you have heard of elsewhere.

Activity Two: Work in groups and discuss the following questions.

1. What are the different kinds of disasters? How are they formed?
2. In recent years, there have been more and more natural disasters causing much damage to the human life. What human factors contribute to the increasing number of disasters?

Activity Three: Problems and Solutions

A disaster, whether a natural one or a human-made hazard, will surely have a negative impact on society and the environment. Developing countries around the world suffer great losses when a disaster hits—more than 95 percent of all deaths caused by disasters occur in developing countries, and losses due to natural disasters are 20 times greater (as a percentage of GDP) in developing countries than in industrialized countries.

Unit 5 Disasters

Work in groups to simulate a conference based on the following situation: leaders from both developing countries and developed countries are holding a summit conference to discuss solutions to the problems that a disaster brings to developing countries.

Writing Practice

Letter Writing: A Letter of Notice

Write a letter to all of the students in the English Department, notifying them of the coming sandstorm and the necessary measures they should take.

> 23 March, 20____
>
> Dear all,
>
>
>
> The Students' Union

Composition Writing

Write a composition within 120 words on the human factors contributing to global warming and the various kinds of disasters which may result from it. Provide viable solutions at the end of your composition.

Unit 6 Legends and Myths

Warm-up Activities

1. Describe yourself as a mythical character or creature. Let the rest of the class guess who you are. For example, I am half woman, half fish living in the sea. What am I?
2. How do ancient myths or fables relate to people today? For instance, some characters in Greek mythology are still in people's everyday speech.

Text I

Modern Mythology

Pre-reading Questions

1. What comes to your mind when modern mythology is mentioned?
2. Why do people create new myths in modern times?

1   Not all mythology dates from the days of ancient cultures. People around the world continue to create new myths and to embroider or rework existing ones. Modern technologies such as publishing, movies, telecommunications, and the Internet allow folktales, rumors, and newly minted myths to travel faster and reach more people than ever before. One distinctive feature of some modern legends is that they originated as artistic creations, although their creators may have drawn on earlier themes.

2   Like all myths and legends, modern mythology springs from a sense of life's wonder, excitement, mystery, and terror. Modern legends offer images of

Unit 6   Legends and Myths

the best and worst aspects of the human condition. They suggest that good behavior will be rewarded and evil, greedy, or foolish behavior punished. Some modern legends reflect people's fear of rapid social change or of science and technology; others appeal to their desire to find meaningful patterns beneath the confusing chaos of ordinary life.

3   A number of modern myths explore what it means to be human. In 1912 the American writer Edgar Rice Burroughs created the character Tarzan, the son of an English nobleman raised by apes in the African jungle. Like earlier myths about people raised by animals, the Tarzan story features animals with admirable "human" qualities and people with brutish "animal" qualities. Tarzan himself combines the virtues of animal strength and civilized honor.

4   Like the heroes of ancient myths, modern superheroes have extraordinary powers. The most famous superhero is Superman, created by American cartoonists Jerry Siegel and Joseph Shuster in 1938. In comics and on radio, television, and movie screens, he fights for "truth, justice, and the American way," using his powers of flight and incredible strength, powers he possesses because he is from another planet. Like most modern superheroes, Superman keeps his identity a secret and pretends to be an ordinary man. Such myths suggest that anyone can have unsuspected potential for heroism.

5   If Tarzan and Superman offer visions of the ideal human being, the legend of Frankenstein explores human flaws. The English writer Marry Wollstonecraft Shelly wrote Frankenstein, or, the Modern Prometheus in 1818. It tells the story of Victor Frankenstein, a scientist who builds an artificial creature from pieces of corpses and brings the creature to life. An element of the Frankenstein story that has been repeated in many modern books and movies is the theme of the "mad scientist" who crosses a moral boundary and unleashes forces beyond his control. The monster, who is intelligent and kind but so ugly that everyone fears and hates him, represents everyone who is misunderstood and cannot find a

place in the world. He symbolizes both a fear of the unknown and the pain caused by prejudice.

6   Many ancient myths feature monstrous, frightening beings who are partly human and who prey on humans. Such figures continue to fascinate today. Among the most enduring monsters in modern mythology are werewolves and vampires. The werewolves represent the idea that a fearsome beast lurks inside a human being; vampires give form to humans' fears of darkness and death. One of the most famous vampires is Count Dracula from the 1897 novel *Dracula* by Irish writer Bram Stoker. A modern twist on the vampire legend emerged in the 1990s, when a few books, films, and television shows portrayed vampires as sympathetic characters battling against their bloodthirsty impulses.

7   A great many modern myths attempt to paint the world in dramatic colors or find hidden meanings in random events. Once they have appeared in print a few times, such myths begin to seem like facts to some people. "The curse of King Tutankhamen's tomb," for example, was a fiction coined by newspaper writers, but it gave rise to a body of tales about ancient mummies coming to life to attack people who disturb their tombs.

8   One of the most widespread legends of modern times concerns UFOs, unidentified flying objects or flying saucers. Ever since pilot Kenneth Arnold reported seeing strange objects flying over the state of Washington in 1947, rumors and reports of spacecraft piloted by extraterrestrial beings have surfaced in the media. By the late 1990s, the UFO myth had grown into an elaborate set of stories about various kinds of aliens, some of which kidnap humans. UFO stories bear striking similarities to earlier myths, such as kidnappings by fairies and mysterious appearances of ghosts or demons. Ironically, the lack of reliable evidence to support UFO claims merely adds to the mythology, as people maintain that the absence of evidence points to a government conspiracy or cover-up. Conspiracies—secret forces that shape events and conceal the truth from the public—appear in a number of modern myths, perhaps reflecting a failure of trust in leaders and authority figures.

9   The search for the marvelous and strange lies behind many modern legends. Stories about mysterious unknown creatures, such as Sasquatch or Bigfoot in North America and the yeti or Abominable Snowman in the Himalayas, are survivors of ancient folklore taken seriously by some modern believers. Other myths—such as the notion that an unusually large number of

Unit 6 Legends and Myths

deaths and disappearances have occurred in a region of the Atlantic Ocean known as the Bermuda Triangle—are modern inventions. Many such legends have mysterious and inexplicable elements in place of the gods and magic of earlier mythologies.

10   The fact that the generation of myths has been and remains such an enduring feature of human behaviour perhaps suggests that people need to create something beyond the ordinary, to answer the puzzles of existence, to explain the unexplainable. Why, we might ask, are people so often willing to believe some myths, even when they have been clearly proven for what they are? Are people basically gullible? Are they too slow to apply logical analysis? Or can we put it down to another age-old human characteristic which applies across cultures—the sheer enjoyment of a good story?

(889 words)

Words and Expressions

mythology	/mɪˈθɒlədʒɪ/	n.	set of ancient myths 神话（总称）
myth	/mɪθ/	n.	an ancient story, especially one invented in order to explain natural or historical events （古代的）神话
embroider	/ɪmˈbrɔɪdə/	vt.	to make a story or report of events more interesting or exciting by adding details that are not true 对（故事或报道）加以渲染
telecommunication	/ˌtelɪkəˌmjuːnɪˈkeɪʃən/	n.	the sending and receiving of messages by telephone, radio, television, etc. 电信
mint	/mɪnt/	vt.	to invent new words, phrases, or ideas 创造，发明
draw on			to use 利用，动用
spring from			to arise from 由……引起
mystery	/ˈmɪstərɪ/	n.	something strange or unknown which has not yet been explained or understood 神秘的事物，谜
evil	/ˈiːvəl/	adj.	immoral, cruel, or very unpleasant 邪恶的

confusing	/kənˈfjuːzɪŋ/	adj.	unclear and difficult to understand 令人困惑的，含糊不清的
chaos	/ˈkeɪɒs/	n.	a state of total confusion and lack of order 无秩序状态
nobleman	/ˈnəʊblmən/	n.	a man who is a member of a high social class and has a title such as 'Duke' (男)贵族
ape	/eɪp/	n.	an animal that is similar to a monkey but has no tail or only a very short tail 猿
brutish	/ˈbruːtɪʃ/	adj.	cruel and not sensitive to people's feelings 兽性的，没有人性的
superhero	/ˈsuːpəˌhɪərəʊ/	n.	a character in stories who uses special powers, such as great strength or the ability to fly, to help people 超级英雄
cartoonist	/kɑːˈtuːnɪst/	n.	someone who draws cartoons 漫画家
comic	/ˈkɒmɪk/	n.	a magazine for children that tells a story using cartoon strips (儿童)连环漫画杂志
incredible	/ɪnˈkredɪbəl/	adj.	extremely good, large, or great 极大的，极好的
heroism	/ˈherəʊɪzəm/	n.	very great courage 英雄气概
vision	/ˈvɪʒən/	n.	an idea of what you think something should be like 看法，观点
flaw	/flɔː/	n.	a mistake, mark, or weakness that makes something imperfect 缺点，瑕疵
corpse	/kɔːps/	n.	the dead body of a person 尸体
unleash	/ʌnˈliːʃ/	vt.	to suddenly let a strong force, feeling, etc. have its full effect 释放出
monster	/ˈmɒnstə/	n.	an imaginary or ancient creature that is large, ugly, and frightening 怪兽，怪物
symbolize	/ˈsɪmbəlaɪz/	vt.	to represent 象征
monstrous	/ˈmɒnstrəs/	adj.	unusually large and often frightening 异常大的
prey on			to hunt and eat 捕食
fascinate	/ˈfæsɪneɪt/	vi./vt.	to attract or interest someone very much 吸引
enduring	/ɪnˈdjʊərɪŋ/	adj.	continuing for a very long time 持久的
werewolf	/ˈweəwʊlf/	n.	a person who, in stories, changes into a wolf every month when the moon is full 狼人
vampire	/ˈvæmpaɪə/	n.	in stories, a dead person that sucks people's blood by biting their necks 吸血鬼

Unit 6 Legends and Myths

fearsome	/ˈfɪəsəm/	*adj.*	very frightening 可怕的
lurk	/lɜːk/	*vt.*	to exist although it is not always noticeable 暗藏，潜藏
emerge	/ɪˈmɜːdʒ/	*vt.*	to begin to be known or noticed 兴起
portray	/pɔːˈtreɪ/	*vt.*	to describe or represent something or someone 描绘
bloodthirsty	/ˈblʌdθɜːstɪ/	*adj.*	eager to kill and wound, or enjoying killing and violence 嗜杀成性的
impulse	/ˈɪmpʌls/	*n.*	a sudden strong desire to do something 冲动
dramatic	/drəˈmætɪk/	*adj.*	intended to be impressive, so that people notice 惹人注目的
curse	/kɜːs/	*n.*	a word or sentence used to ask God or a magical power to do something bad to someone or something 诅咒，咒语
coin	/kɔɪn/	*vt.*	to invent a new word or expression, especially one that many people start to use 创造，杜撰（新词语等）
give rise to			to be the reason why something happens, especially something bad or unpleasant 引起（导致）某事
mummy	/ˈmʌmɪ/	*n.*	a dead body that has been preserved by wrapping it in cloth, especially in ancient Egypt（尤指古埃及的）木乃伊
pilot	/ˈpaɪlət/	*vt.*	to guide an aircraft, spacecraft, or ship as its pilot 驾驶（飞机或宇宙飞船）
		n.	a person who is licensed to operate an aircraft in flight 飞行员，领航员
extraterrestrial	/ˌekstrətəˈrestrɪəl/	*adj.*	relating to things that exist outside the earth 地球外的
surface	/ˈsɜːfɪs/	*vi.*	to become known about or easy to notice 被公开，显露
elaborate	/ɪˈlæbərət/	*adj.*	having a lot of small parts or details put together in a complicated way 详尽的，精心制作的
alien	/ˈeɪljən/	*n.*	in stories, a creature from another world 外星人（生物）
kidnap	/ˈkɪdnæp/	*vt.*	to take someone somewhere illegally by force,

			often in order to get money for returning them 绑架
demon	/'diːmən/	n.	an evil spirit or force 魔鬼
conspiracy	/kən'spɪrəsɪ/	n.	a secret plan made by two or more people to do something that is harmful or illegal 阴谋，密谋
cover-up	/'kʌvərʌp/	n.	an attempt to prevent the public from discovering the truth about something 隐瞒，掩饰
conceal	/kən'siːl/	vt.	to hide something carefully 掩盖，隐藏
marvelous	/'mɑːvələs/	adj.	extremely good, enjoyable, impressive, etc. 极好的，绝妙的
yeti	/'jetɪ/	n.	a large hairy creature like a human which some people believe lives in the Himalayan mountains 雪人
Abominable Snowman			(据传生活在喜马拉雅山一带的)雪人
the Himalayas	/ˌhɪmə'leɪəz/		喜马拉雅山脉
survivor	/sə'vaɪvə/	n.	someone who continues to live after others have died 幸存者
notion	/'nəʊʃən/	n.	an idea, belief, or opinion 观点，概念，看法
inexplicable	/ˌɪnɪk'splɪkəbəl/	adj.	too unusual or strange to be explained or understood 无法解释的，费解的
gullible	/'gʌlɪbəl/	adj.	too ready to believe what other people tell you, so that you are easily tricked 轻信的，易上当的；易受骗的

Notes:

Prometheus In Greek mythology, Prometheus is a Titan known for his wily intelligence, who stole fire from Zeus and gave it to mortals for their use. He was then punished for his crime by Zeus.

Tutankhamen (1341 B.C.–1323 B.C.) was an Egyptian Pharaoh of the Eighteenth dynasty. The 1922 discovery of Tutankhamen's intact tomb received worldwide press coverage and sparked a renewed public interest in ancient Egypt.

Bermuda Triangle also known as the Devil's Triangle, is a region of the northwestern Atlantic Ocean in which a number of aircraft and surface vessels have disappeared.

Unit 6　Legends and Myths

Reading Comprehension

I.　**Explain the following terms with the information you read from the text.**

Mythology:

_____

Tarzan:

_____

Superman:

_____

UFO:

_____

Tutankhamen:

_____

II.　**Answer the following questions.**
1. What has made myths travel faster?
2. What does Superman fight for and how does he manage to fight for his goals?
3. What does Frankenstein symbolize?
4. What do werewolf and vampire stand for respectively?
5. According to some fictions, what will happen if one disturbs the tombs of mummies?
6. What has happened in the region of the Bermuda Triangle? What is your attitude towards the happenings in this area?

III.　**Judge, according to the text, whether the following statements are true or false. For false statements, write the facts in parentheses.**
1. All mythology dates back to the times of ancient cultures.
   (   )
2. Modern mythology springs from a sense of life's wonder, excitement, mystery and terror, which is quite different from other myths and legends.
   (   )
3. One of the most famous superheroes in modern mythology is Superman.
   (   )

4. Most of the modern superheroes keep their identities secret.
   (   )

5. Among the most enduring monsters in ancient mythology are werewolves and vampires.
   (   )

6. An element of the Frankenstein story is the theme of "mad scientist".
   (   )

7. By the early 1990s, the UFO myth had grown into stories of aliens.
   (   )

IV. Paraphrase the following sentences within the context.

1. (Para. 1) One distinctive feature of some modern legends is that they originated as artistic creations, although their creators may have drawn on earlier themes.

2. (Para. 5) An element of the Frankenstein story that has been repeated in many modern books and movies is the theme of the "mad scientist" who crosses a moral boundary and unleashes forces beyond his control.

3. (Para. 6) A modern twist on the vampire legend emerged in the 1990s, when a few books, films, and television shows portrayed vampires as sympathetic characters battling against their bloodthirsty impulses.

4. (Para. 7) "The curse of King Tutankhamen's tomb", for example, was a fiction coined by newspaper writers, but it gave rise to a body of tales about ancient mummies coming to life to attack people who disturb their tombs.

5. (Para. 8) Ironically, the lack of reliable evidence to support UFO claims merely adds to the mythology, as people maintain that the absence of evidence points to a government conspiracy or cover-up.

Unit 6 Legends and Myths

Vocabulary Exercises

I. Fill in the blank in each sentence with a word or phrase taken from the box in its appropriate form.

> embroider   mint   unleash   conspiracy   unsuspected
> portray   spring from lurk   prey (up)on give rise to
> inexplicable   elaborate

1. His _____ of Islamic culture in this newspaper is really fascinating.
2. It was very dark that night, so she didn't see the figure _____ behind the bushes.
3. Naturally, the author _____ the tale a little to make it more interesting and exciting.
4. It is always the case that strong animals _____ weaker ones in the animal world.
5. Rachel's arrival at his birthday party had _____ passions in him that he could barely control.
6. Her need to be recognized and liked obviously _____ a deep-rooted insecurity.
7. Don't blame him. Under the circumstances, what he said was quite _____.
8. Your improper words will _____ doubts concerning your true intentions.
9. Her best friends are making the most _____ preparations for her wedding.
10. The phrase was _____ for that special occasion.
11. Make sure to use the safety belt to protect yourself from any _____ injury.
12. He believes that there was a _____ to keep him out of the committee.

II. Choose a word or phrase that best completes each of the following sentences.

1. Do you know what lies _____ their decision?
   A. down   B. in   C. behind   D. up
2. The Olympic Games _____ in 776 B.C. in Olympia, a small town in Greece.
   A. originated   B. stemmed   C. derived   D. descended
3. Jerry thought he was innocent, so he appealed _____ the high court _____ his sentence.
   A. up; against   B. on; about   C. to; against   D. to; about
4. Some people can never go above 4000 meters because their bodies are unable to _____ these extreme conditions.
   A. adopt to   B. adapt to   C. apply to   D. appeal to
5. Although she often seems quite cold and harsh, her smiling eyes _____ her true nature.
   A. betray   B. tell   C. conceal   D. hide
6. I've always _____ my uncle for his courage and determination.
   A. held on to   B. lived up to   C. gave rise to   D. looked up to

Translation Exercises

Translate each of the following sentences into English, using the word or phrase given in the brackets.

1. 据英国媒体报道，世界上有史可考的最古老的笑话可追溯到公元前1900年。(date from)

2. 文艺复兴时期，很多文学家对古希腊罗马神话产生了浓厚兴趣，并经常引用这些神话故事作为创作素材。(draw on)

3. 以前我们所犯的错误都是粗心大意造成的，为了避免类似错误再次发生，我们要谨慎行事。(spring from)

4. 市长在发表就职演说时呼吁市民鼎力支持这项健身运动,建设一个充满活力的宜居城市。(appeal to)

5. 野狼常常在农忙季节潜入农民家里,捕食他们的孩子。(prey on)

6. 医疗事故发生后,他企图用谎言掩盖自己的错误,但谎言最终被事实揭穿。(cover up)

7. 作为事故的目击者,他被指控接受肇事者的贿赂,并向警方隐瞒真相。(conceal from)

Text II

Prometheus Steals Fire
—A Myth of Ancient Greeks

Pre-reading Questions

1. Have you heard of some Chinese myths? Who brought Fire to the humans in Chinese myths?
2. Who is Prometheus? What did he do for the humans?

1　　One of the oddest themes in mythology is that of the theft of fire. It crosses cultures and eras, and turns up almost everywhere. The story of Prometheus is perhaps the best known of these theft-of-fire myths to Westerners, though not that many are likely to know the background story, or that Prometheus is as much or more a trickster who takes on Zeus himself as he is a symbol of heroic defiance.

2　　Prometheus was not truly one of the gods of Mount Olympus. He was a Titan, born from the union of the Titan Lapetus and the nymph

Asia. It was Lapetus who had led an unsuccessful revolt against the gods, and one of Prometheus' brothers, Atlas, wound up carrying the weight of the world as a punishment after that.

3 But Prometheus had not revolted. And so when Zeus, king of the gods, was smitten by a terrible headache, it was Prometheus who was trusted to help him. The help took the form of striking Zeus on the head so that the goddess Athena could be born, fully grown, from his forehead.

4 Not long after this strange event Prometheus and his brother Epimetheus traveled down from Olympus to the Greek province of Boitia. There they looked around at the lovely landscape. But it needed something. So the two Titans made a series of clay figures and showed them to Athena. She breathed life into the figures that Prometheus had created, and they became human beings who honored him. The figures that his brother Epimetheus had created became animals, which attacked him.

5 Zeus was furious. How dare these upstarts interfere with his divine rights? He forbade Prometheus from teaching humanity any of the ways of civilization.

6 Athena didn't approve. She ignored what Zeus was ordering, and taught Prometheus so that he might teach humanity.

7 Fuming, Zeus demanded that humanity make sacrifices to the gods to show that they were properly obedient and worshipful. The humans went to Prometheus to ask what belonged to them and what belonged to the gods.

8 Prometheus told them to sacrifice an ox, then divide the sacrifice into two bags. In the first bag they were to put the bones, and place the fat from the ox on top to hide them. In the second bag, they were to put the meat, and place the ox's intestines on top to hide that as well.

9 Prometheus called to Zeus so that he might choose which portion of the sacrifice would be his. Zeus, seeing the fat in the first bag, assumed that it must also contain the meat, so he chose that one—ending up with the bones of the ox as the sacrifice.

10 Now Zeus was truly furious. He would not let humanity thrive! So he forbade any of the gods to let humanity have the gift of fire.

11 Prometheus was angry as well. If fire was denied to humanity, the humans could never be more than animals. Zeus had set guards at the entrance to Olympus, but Athena secretly told Prometheus about an unguarded back entrance into Olympus.

Unit 6 Legends and Myths

12   So Prometheus sneaked into Olympus that night through the back entrance and stole his way to the chariot of the sun. Fires forever burned there, and Prometheus quickly lit a torch, then extinguished it and hid the hot coals in a fennel stalk so no flames would be seen. He hurried down Mount Olympus to the humans and gave them the gift of the fire.

13   Now all of Zeus' fury was centered on Prometheus. He created the lovely Pandora and gave her a box into which Zeus had placed all the evil of the world, then sent Pandora and her box to Prometheus as a gift from Zeus himself.

14   Prometheus instantly saw the curse that Pandora and her box carried. He refused the gift, giving it instead to his brother Epimetheus. It was Epimetheus who opened the box and released the evils upon the world—although he also released hope as well.

15   Zeus no longer tried stealth. Prometheus was captured and chained to a rock in the Caucasus Mountains, where a great eagle would eat his liver every day, leaving only at nightfall. Then the liver would grow back, in time for the eagle's return the next day.

16   Zeus offered to free Prometheus if he would tell Zeus the details of the prophecy that told of Zeus' dethroning. But Prometheus refused.

17   At last the half-god hero Heracles freed Prometheus from the rock. Zeus' order had stated that Prometheus be bound to the rock for the rest of eternity, but Prometheus and Heracles solved that problem. Heracles simply broke off a link of the chains, set it with a chip of the rock, and gave it to Prometheus to wear.

18   From that day on, men began to wear rings with stones and gems set into them to honor Prometheus for what he had undergone on their behalf. And even to this day, the name of Prometheus has come to stand for the strength that withstands all oppression.

(840 words)

Reading Comprehension

I. **Answer the following questions with the information you read from the passage.**

1. How was the goddess Athena born?
2. Who created human beings and animals? What did Zeus think of it?

3. How did Prometheus help humans make sacrifices to the gods?
4. How did Prometheus steal fire from Olympus and give humans the gift of fire?
5. Who is Pandora? What was in Pandora's Box?
6. How was Prometheus punished? And who freed him from the rock?

II. **Topics for discussion and reflection.**

1. Where do myths come from? How do people pass myths down from generation to generation?
2. Have you read any Chinese books on myths, such as *Shan Hai Jing*? Find some Chinese myths and compare them with the Greek ones to learn the cultural differences behind the myths.

Exercises for Integrated Skills

I. **Dictation**

Listen to the following passage. Altogether the passage will be read to you four times. During the first reading, which will be read at normal speed, listen and try to understand the meaning. For the second and third readings, the passage will be read sentence by sentence, or phrase by phrase, with intervals of 15 to 20 seconds. The last reading will be done at normal speed again and during this time you should check your work. You will then be given 2 minutes to check through your work once more.

Unit 6 Legends and Myths

II. Cloze

Fill in each blank in the passage below with a word or phrase taken from the box in its appropriate form.

companion	maintain	plunge	disturb	action
miracle	advantage	plead	pretty	considerable
procession	name	charm	bear	supreme
appear	argue	punish	rush	prior

As the sky god, Zeus had easy access to the women of the world and took full __1__ of it. Also, his power as a __2__ god made him difficult to resist. __3__ to his marriage to Hera he was married first to Metis, then Themis. He was interested in Demeter but she resisted him. His third wife was Mnemosyne. The list of lovers after his marriage, to Hera, is __4__.

Europa was the daughter of the King Agenor of Sidon. She had the continent of Europe named for her. Somewhat __5__ Hera was distracted during her affair with Zeus and never __6__ her for it.

One night Europa had a dream. In this dream two continents, which were in the forms of women, were __7__ over Europa. Asia __8__ that since Europa had been born in Asia she belonged to it. The other continent, which was __9__, said that her birth was not important, that Zeus would give her to it.

It was early morning, __10__ by the dream Europa did not go back to sleep. She summoned her __11__, who were all daughters of nobility and of her age. It was a beautiful day and they went off gathering flowers by the sea. Zeus noticed this __12__ group, particularly Europa, who was the __13__ of all the maidens. Some says that Eros induced him into __14__ with one of his darts, although Zeus often had enough self-motivation. In any case, Zeus __15__ to the group as a white bull. A white bull is more beautiful than any other. A bull so obviously gentle that all the maidens __16__ to stroke and pet it.

The bull lay down in front of Europa. She slid on to its back. Instantly, the bull charged off, __17__ into the sea, and began to swim rapidly from the shore. Europa saw that a __18__ had joined them, Nereids riding dolphins, Triton blowing his horn, even Poseidon. From this she realized that the bull must be a god. She __19__ with him to pity her. Zeus spoke to her and explained

his love. He took her to Crete, where he had been raised. He promised that she would ___20___ him many famous sons. Her sons included Minos I and Rhadamanthus.

Oral Activities

Work in groups and discuss the following questions.

1. What is the social significance of the myths and legends to the modern society? If people read them merely for entertainment, will myths and legends fade out in the future?
2. Why are legends and myths important in people's lives? What kind of resources might become legends or myths?

Writing Practice

Letter Writing: A Letter of Refusal

Your friend Mary invites you to attend a lecture on Greek Mythology and the Olympics. But unfortunately you are to have a debate contest on the same day. Write an informal letter to decline the offer politely.

23 April, 20____

Dear Mary,

With love,
John

Composition Writing

Write a composition about your favorite mythic or legendary story in about 120 words. The reason(s) why you like the myth most should be included in the composition.

Unit 7 Shopping

Warm-up Activities

1. How has shopping evolved during the past few decades? Conduct a survey among people of different ages and report your findings to the class.
2. How does shopping differ in different areas? Ask people from a foreign country, a remote area and a modern city about their shopping experiences. Draw a conclusion from your findings.
3. Role play: Let's go Shopping

   Below is the store directory of a shopping mall. Work in groups to act out the following situation. Some of the members act as shop assistants or waiters/waitresses in any of the following stores. The rest act as customers and make a shopping list.

Name/Brand	Category
Apple	Electronics, Computers and Telephones
Esprit	Women's Apparel
Disney Store	Toys, Hobbies and Pets
Indigo Books & Music	Books & News, Music & Videos
McDonald's	Fast Food
Mrs. Field's Cookies	Specialty Foods
Nike	Sporting Goods & Athletic Wear
Panache	Fashion Accessories
Shopper's Drug Mart	Pharmacies and Drug

Text I

A Pair of Silk Stockings (I)

> **Pre-reading Questions**
>
> 1. What is your first reaction to the title of the text? What do you think the article is about?
> 2. If you happened to win 5 million dollars, what would you like to manage the money?

1   Little Mrs. Sommers one day found herself the *unexpected* possessor of fifteen dollars. It seemed to her a very large amount of money, and the way in which it *stuffed* and *bulged* her worn old *porte-monnaie* gave her a feeling of importance such as she had not enjoyed for years.

2   The question of investment was one that occupied her greatly. For a day or two she walked about *apparently* in a dreamy state, but really absorbed in *speculation* and calculation. She did not wish to act *hastily*, to do anything she might afterwards regret. But it was during the still hours of the night when she lay awake *revolving plans in her mind* that she seemed to see her way clearly toward a proper and *judicious* use of the money.

3   A dollar or two should be added to the price usually paid for Janie's shoes, which would insure their lasting an *appreciable* time longer than they usually did. She would buy so and so many yards of percale for new shirtwaists for the boys and Janie and Mag. She had intended to make the old ones do by skillful *patching*. Mag should have another *gown*. She had seen some beautiful patterns, *veritable* bargains in the shop windows. And still there would be left enough for new stockings—two pairs *apiece*—and what *darning* that would save for a while! She would get caps for the boys and sailor hats for the girls. The vision of her little *brood* looking fresh and *dainty* and new for

once in their lives excited her and made her restless and wakeful with anticipation.

4   The neighbors sometimes talked of certain "better days" that little Mrs. Sommers had known before she had ever thought of being Mrs. Sommers. She herself indulged in no such morbid retrospection. She had no time—no second of time to devote to the past. The needs of the present absorbed her every faculty. A vision of the future like some dim, gaunt monster sometimes appalled her, but luckily tomorrow never comes.

5   Mrs. Sommers was one who knew the value of bargains; who could stand for hours making her way inch by inch toward the desired object that was selling below cost. She could elbow her way if need be; she had learned to clutch a piece of goods and hold it and stick to it with persistence and determination till her turn came to be served, no matter when it came.

6   But that day she was a little faint and tired. She had swallowed a light luncheon—no! when she came to think of it, between getting the children fed and the place righted, and preparing herself for the shopping bout, she had actually forgotten to eat any luncheon at all!

7   She sat herself upon a revolving stool before a counter that was comparatively deserted, trying to gather strength and courage to charge through an eager multitude that was besieging breastworks of shirting and figured lawn. An all-gone limp feeling had come over her and she rested her hand aimlessly upon the counter. She wore no gloves. By degrees she grew aware that her hand had encountered something very soothing, very pleasant to touch. She looked down to see that her hand lay upon a pile of silk stockings. A placard nearby announced that they had been reduced in price from two dollars and fifty cents to one dollar and ninety-eight cents; and a young girl who stood behind the counter asked her if she wished to examine their line of silk hosiery. She smiled just as if she had been asked to inspect a tiara of diamonds with the ultimate view of purchasing it. But she went on feeling the soft, sheeny luxurious things—with both hands now, holding them up to see them glisten, and to feel them glide serpent-like through her fingers.

8   Two hectic blotches came suddenly into her pale cheeks. She looked up at the girl.

9   "Do you think there are any eights-and-a-half among these?"

10   There were any number of eights-and-a-half. In fact, there were more of that size than any other. Here was a light-blue pair; there were some lavender, some all black and various shades of tan and gray. Mrs. Sommers selected a black pair and looked at them very long and closely. She pretended to be examining their texture, which the clerk assured her was excellent.

11   "A dollar and ninety-eight cents," she mused aloud. "Well, I'll take this pair." She handed the girl a five-dollar bill and waited for her change and for her parcel. What a very small parcel it was! It seemed lost in the depths of her shabby old shopping-bag.

12   Mrs. Sommers after that did not move in the direction of the bargain counter. She took the elevator, which carried her to an upper floor into the region of the ladies' waiting-rooms. Here, in a retired corner, she exchanged her cotton stockings for the new silk ones which she had just bought. She was not going through any acute mental process or reasoning with herself, nor was she striving to explain to her satisfaction the motive of her action. She was not thinking at all. She seemed for the time to be taking a rest from that laborious and fatiguing function and to have abandoned herself to some mechanical impulse that directed her actions and freed her of responsibility.

13   How good was the touch of the raw silk to her flesh! She felt like lying back in the cushioned chair and reveling for a while in the luxury of it. She did for a little while. Then she replaced her shoes, rolled the cotton stockings together and thrust them into her bag. After doing this she crossed straight over to the shoe department and took her seat to be fitted.

14   She was fastidious. The clerk could not make her out; he could not reconcile her shoes with her stockings, and she was not too easily pleased. She held back her skirts and turned her feet one way and her head another way as she glanced down at the polished, pointed-tipped boots. Her feet and ankles looked very pretty. She could not realize that they belonged to her and were a part of herself. She wanted an excellent and stylish fit, she told the young fellow who served her, and she did not mind the difference of a dollar or two more in the price so long as she got what she desired.

(1,087 words)

Unit 7　Shopping

Words and Expressions

unexpected	/ˌʌnɪksˈpektɪd/	adj.	used to describe something that is surprising because you were not expecting it 意外的，想不到的
stuff	/stʌf/	vt.	to fill something until it is full 装满
bulge	/bʌldʒ/	vi.	to stick out in a rounded shape, especially because something is very full or too tight 鼓起
porte-monnaie		n.	零钱包
apparently	/əˈpærəntlɪ/	adv.	clearly, obviously 显然，看起来
speculation	/ˌspekjʊˈleɪʃən/	n.	when you guess about the possible causes or effects of something without knowing all the facts, or the guesses that you make 猜测，推测
hastily	/ˈheɪstɪlɪ/	adv.	quickly, perhaps too quickly 仓促地，匆忙地
revolve something in one's mind			仔细考虑某事物
judicious	/dʒuˈdɪʃəs/	adj.	done in a sensible and careful way 明智的，审慎的
appreciable	/əˈpriːʃəbəl/	adj.	large enough to be noticed or considered important 明显的，可觉察到的
patch	/pætʃ/	vt.	to repair a hole in something by putting a piece of something else over it 缝补（衣服等）
gown	/gaʊn/	n.	a women's dress, especially a long one for special occasions 女服（尤指特殊场合穿的长外衣）
veritable	/ˈverɪtəbəl/	adj.	real 真正的，名副其实的
apiece	/əˈpiːs/	adv.	costing or having a particular amount each 每件，每个，每人
darning	/ˈdɑːnɪŋ/	n.	the repairing of holes in clothing by stitching them with thread 缝补，织补
brood	/bruːd/	n.	a family with a lot of children 有许多孩子的家庭
dainty	/ˈdeɪntɪ/	adj.	small, pretty, and delicate 精致的，小巧的
restless	/ˈrestlɪs/	adj.	characterized by or manifesting unrest especially of mind 不安定的，躁动不安的
anticipation	/ænˌtɪsɪˈpeɪʃən/	n.	a feeling of excitement about something that is going to happen in the near future 期望，预期，预料

indulge	/ɪnˈdʌldʒ/	vt.	to let oneself to enjoy the pleasure of something 让自己尽情享受某事物
morbid	/ˈmɔːbɪd/	adj.	with a strong and unhealthy interest in unpleasant subjects, especially death 病态的，不健康的
retrospection	/ˌretrəˈspekʃən/	n.	thinking about the past 回想，回顾
faculty	/ˈfækəltɪ/	n.	a natural ability, such as the ability to see, hear, or think clearly 能力
dim	/dɪm/	adj.	not easy to be seen because it is too far away, or there is not enough light 模糊的，看不清楚的
gaunt	/gɔːnt/	adj.	looking very ugly 丑陋的，难看的
appall	/əˈpɔːl/	vt.	to make someone feel very shocked and upset 使惊骇
clutch	/klʌtʃ/	vt.	to take or try to take hold of something tightly, usually in fear, anxiety or pain 紧握，紧抓
faint	/feɪnt/	adj.	feeling weak and as if you are about to become unconscious 虚弱的，像要昏厥的
right	/raɪt/	vt.	to put something back into the state or situation that it should be in 使回复到适当的、正确的位置
bout	/baʊt/	n.	a short period of time during which you do something a lot, especially something that is bad for you 一回，一阵，一场，一番
comparatively	/kəmˈpærətɪvlɪ/	adv.	as compared to something else or to a previous state 相对地，比较地
deserted	/dɪˈzɜːtɪd/	adj.	empty and quiet because no people are there 被遗弃的，被舍弃的
charge through			冲过，奔过
multitude	/ˈmʌltɪtjuːd/	n.	a very large number of ordinary people in a particular place or situation 大众，民众
besiege	/bɪˈsiːdʒ/	vt.	to surround somebody or something closely 围住
breastwork	/ˈbrestwɜːk/	n.	fortification consisting of a low wall 矮防护墙；齐胸高
shirting	/ˈʃɜːtɪŋ/	n.	any of various fabrics used to make men's

Unit 7 Shopping

			shirts 衬衫料子
figured	/ˈfɪɡəd/	adj.	decorated with a small pattern 有花纹的, 饰有图案的
lawn	/lɔːn/	n.	a fine cloth made from cotton or linen 上等细棉布, 细麻布
limp	/lɪmp/	adj.	not firm or strong 弱的, 软的
come over			(强烈情感)突然袭向(某人)
placard	/ˈplækɑːd/	n.	a large notice or advertisement on a piece of card, which is put up or carried in a public place 广告牌, 布告
hosiery	/ˈhəʊzjərɪ/	n.	a general word for tights, stockings, or socks, used in shops and in the clothing industry 袜类(用于商店及成衣业中)
sheeny	/ˈʃiːnɪ/	adj.	lustrous, glistening 光亮的, 有光泽的
luxurious	/lʌɡˈzjʊərɪəs/	adj.	very expensive, beautiful, and comfortable 奢华的, 华丽的
glisten	/ˈɡlɪsən/	vi.	to shine and look wet or oily 闪光, 闪耀
serpent	/ˈsɜːpənt/	n.	a snake, especially a large one 蛇(尤指大蛇)
hectic	/ˈhektɪk/	adj.	very pink 粉色的
blotch	/blɒtʃ/	n.	a pink or red mark on the skin, or a coloured mark on something 斑, 疤, 污渍
lavender	/ˈlævɪndə/	n.	a pale purple colour 浅紫色
tan	/tæn/	n.	a light yellowish-brown colour 棕黄色, 黄褐色
texture	/ˈtekstʃə/	n.	the way a surface or material feels when you touch it, especially how smooth or rough it is 质地, 手感
muse	/mjuːz/	vt.	to say something to oneself in a thoughtful way 沉思自语地说
reasoning	/ˈriːzənɪŋ/	n.	a process of thinking carefully about something in order to make a judgment 推理, 推论
motive	/ˈməʊtɪv/	n.	the reason that makes someone do something, especially when this reason is kept hidden 动机, 原因, 目的
laborious	/ləˈbɔːrɪəs/	adj.	taking a lot of time and effort 缓慢而吃力的
fatiguing	/fəˈtiːɡɪŋ/	adj.	extremely tiring 令人疲惫不堪的
mechanical	/mɪˈkænɪkəl/	adj.	acting (as if) without thinking, in a machine-like way 机械的, 不加思考的

revel	/'revəl/	vi.	to enjoy something very much 尽情享受
thrust	/θrʌst/	vt.	to push something somewhere roughly 猛推,（用力）推
fastidious	/fæs'tɪdɪəs/	adj.	selecting carefully 仔细挑选的
make somebody out			理解（某人的想法、感觉等）
reconcile	/'rekənsaɪl/	vt.	to make (aims, ideas, etc.) agree when they seem to conflict 使一致, 符合, 调和
polished	/'pɒlɪʃt/	adj.	shiny because of being rubbed, usually with polish 擦亮的, 磨光的
stylish	/'staɪlɪʃ/	adj.	attractive in a fashionable way 时髦的, 漂亮的

Reading Comprehension

I. Summarize the text into a few sentences, which indicate the main idea of the article.

_____

_____

II. Answer the following questions.

1. How was Mrs. Sommers occupied by the investment of the fifteen dollars?
2. What did Mrs. Sommers plan to buy with the money? List the items.
3. Did Mrs. Sommers think of the "better days" very often? Why or why not?
4. How did Mrs. Sommers feel before she sat herself upon a revolving stool before a counter? What happened hereafter?
5. Do you think the pair of silk stockings Mrs. Sommers bought was a bargain? Why or why not?
6. Where did Mrs. Sommers go after she bought the silk stockings? And what did she do?
7. Did Mrs. Sommers intend to buy herself a pair of shoes before she went shopping? Why did she go to the shoe department?

Unit 7 Shopping

III. Judge, according to the text, whether the following statements are true or false. For false statements, write the facts in parentheses.

1. The fifteen dollars was given by Mrs. Sommers' husband.
   (   )

2. Mrs. Sommers wanted to make good use of the fifteen dollars.
   (   )

3. Mrs. Sommers planned to buy a new gown for Janie.
   (   )

4. Mrs. Sommers often thought of the "better days" and talked about it with the neighbors.
   (   )

5. Mrs. Sommers was so busy that day that she had actually forgotten to eat any luncheon.
   (   )

6. Mrs. Sommers was charged two dollars and fifty cents for the silk stockings.
   (   )

7. Mrs. Sommers lay back in the cushioned chair and enjoyed herself for quite a long time.
   (   )

IV. Paraphrase the following sentences within the context.

1. (Para. 2) But it was during the still hours of the night when she lay awake revolving plans in her mind that she seemed to see her way clearly toward a proper and judicious use of the money.

2. (Para. 3) The vision of her little brood looking fresh and dainty and new for once in their lives excited her and made her restless and wakeful with anticipation.

3. (Para. 4) She herself indulged in no such morbid retrospection.

4. (Para. 5) She could elbow her way if need be; she had learned to clutch a piece of goods and hold it and stick to it with persistence and determination till her turn came to be served, no matter when it came.

5. (Para. 7) But she went on feeling the soft, sheeny luxurious things—with both hands now, holding them up to see them glisten, and to feel them glide serpent-like through her fingers.

6. (Para. 12) She seemed for the time to be taking a rest from that laborious and fatiguing function and to have abandoned herself to some mechanical impulse that directed her actions and freed her of responsibility.

7. (Para. 14) She was fastidious. The clerk could not make her out; he could not reconcile her shoes with her stockings, and she was not too easily pleased.

Vocabulary Exercises

I. **Fill in each blank with one of the following words from each pair and note the difference of meaning between them. Change the form when necessary.**

1. JUDICIOUS   JUDICIAL
   a. He made a _____ choice to save money for his old age.
   b. The _____ system settles arguments between people.
   c. _____ review was officially recognized in 1803 by the decision of the United States Supreme Court.
   d. Humans should make _____ use of the natural resources.

Unit 7 Shopping

2. **LABORIOUS   LABORED**
   a. Collecting the raw data for the project proved to be a long and _____ task.
   b. The patient's breathing was heavy and _____.
   c. My father wrote out the list _____ by hand.
   d. The novelette is not bad, but some of the episodes are very _____ .

3. **ACUTE   SHARP**
   a. The problem of poverty is more _____ than first thought in rural areas.
   b. The mountains stood in _____ contrast to the blue sky.
   c. John is suffering from a(n) _____ attack of appendicitis.
   d. Mr. Johnson was a man of _____ wit who always spoke his mind.

II. **Fill in the blank in each sentence with a word or phrase taken from the box. Change the form where necessary.**

speculation	veritable	appal(l)	fastidious
make do	come over	reconcile	revel
indulge	in the depth(s) of		

1. I hardly had any food in the house so I just had to _____ with a cup of coffee.
2. His health suffered from _____ in rich food and drink.
3. Laura is _____ in her newly found freedom.
4. You'd better _____ your words with your actions.
5. A wave of sleepiness _____ me and I felt myself sinking fast into a warm and hazy dream.
6. Women are usually _____ about personal hygiene.
7. My garden had become a _____ jungle by the time I came back from the long trip.
8. Teaching such a large group of students is really a(n) _____ difficult job.
9. My father's company was started _____ the recession of the 1930s.
10. Economists and journalists are _____ about whether interest rates will be cut.

III. Choose a word or phrase that best completes each of the following sentences.

1. People _____ that vertical flight transports would carry millions of passengers as do the airliners of today.
   A. convinced   B. anticipated   C. resolved   D. assured

2. I felt _____ to death because I could make nothing of the chairman's speech.
   A. fatigued   B. tired   C. exhausted   D. bored

3. Watching me pulling the calf awkwardly to the barn, the Irish milkmaid fought hard to hold _____ her laughter.
   A. back   B. on   C. out   D. up

4. Although we feel dissatisfied with the election results, we have to become reconciled _____ the decision made by our fellow countrymen.
   A. for   B. on   C. to   D. in

5. If you want to _____ a pleasant visit, find out as much as possible about the manners and customs of your host country.
   A. assure   B. ensure   C. endure   D. insure

6. I couldn't make _____ what the old man was saying.
   A. up   B. out   C. off   D. for

7. Have you come _____ any conclusions about the research project yet?
   A. over   B. on   C. by   D. to

Translation Exercises

Translate each of the following sentences into English, using the word or phrase given in the brackets.

1. 走在人行道上,他全神贯注地想心事,结果撞着了一个行人。(be absorbed in)

2. 人们天天在谈论令人神往的科技王国,但很少有人意识到这些高科技的出现对发展中国家意味着什么。(talk of)

3. 现在仍有许多青少年沉迷于电脑游戏,放学后也不愿意回家。(be indulged in)

4. 春运期间,火车站候车室内拥挤不堪,旅客们不得不在人群中挤着往前走。(elbow one's way)

5. 这家日用电器生产商一直信守对顾客的承诺,在消费者中树立了良好的形象。(stick to)

6. 中国的丝绸通过丝绸之路由陆路运往印度、中东和罗马,用来交换香料和玻璃。(exchange for)

7. 在经历了成功的喜悦与失败的苦涩后,他懂得了如何珍惜现在拥有的一切。(go through)

8. 现代化的家用电器可以使人们从繁琐的日常家务中解脱出来,将精力放到更具挑战性和创造性的工作当中去。(free of)

Text II

A Pair of Silk Stockings (II)

Pre-reading Questions

1. What drives people to purchase items that are not in their original shopping list?
2. To what extent can shopping satisfy people's sense of vanity? Use your personal experience to support your opinion.

1   It was a long time since Mrs. Sommers had been fitted with gloves. On rare occasions when she had bought a pair they were always "bargains," so cheap that it would have been preposterous and unreasonable to have expected them to be fitted to the hand.

2   Now she rested her elbow on the cushion of the glove counter, and a pretty, pleasant young creature, delicate and deft of touch, drew a long-wristed "kid" over Mrs. Sommers's hand. She smoothed it down over the wrist and buttoned it neatly, and both lost themselves for a second or two in admiring contemplation of the little symmetrical gloved hand. But there were other places where money might be spent.

3   There were books and magazines piled up in the window of a stall a few paces down the street. Mrs. Sommers bought two high-priced magazines such as she had been accustomed to read in the days when she had been accustomed to other pleasant things. She carried them without wrappings. As well as she could she lifted her skirts at the crossings. Her stockings and boots and well-fitted gloves had worked marvels in her bearing—had given her a feeling of assurance, a sense of belonging to the well-dressed multitude.

4   She was very hungry. Another time she would have stilled the cravings for food until reaching her own home, where she would have brewed herself a cup of tea and taken a snack of anything that was available. But the impulse that was guiding her would not suffer her to entertain any such thought.

5   There was a restaurant at the corner. She had never entered its doors; from the outside she had sometimes caught glimpses of spotless damask and shining crystal, and soft-stepping waiters serving people of fashion.

6   When she entered her appearance created no surprise, no consternation, as she had half feared it might. She seated herself at a small table alone, and an attentive waiter at once approached to take her order. She did not want a profusion; she craved a nice and tasty bite—a half dozen bluepoints, a plump chop with cress, a something sweet—a *crème-frappée*, for instance; a glass of Rhine wine, and after all a small cup of black coffee.

7   While waiting to be served she removed her gloves very leisurely and laid them beside her. Then she picked up a magazine and glanced through it, cutting the pages with a blunt edge of her knife. It was all very agreeable. The damask was even more spotless than it had seemed through the window, and the crystal

more sparkling. There were quiet ladies and gentlemen, who did not notice her, lunching at the small tables like her own. A soft, pleasing strain of music could be heard, and a gentle breeze, was blowing through the window. She tasted a bite, and she read a word or two, and she sipped the amber wine and wiggled her toes in the silk stockings. The price of it made no difference. She counted the money out to the waiter and left 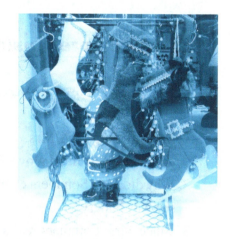 an extra coin on his tray, whereupon he bowed before her as if before a princess of royal blood.

8   There was still money in her purse, and her next temptation presented itself in the shape of a *matinée* poster.

9   It was a little later when she entered the theatre, the play had begun and the house seemed to her to be packed. But there were vacant seats here and there, and into one of them she was ushered, between brilliantly dressed women who had gone there to kill time and eat candy and display their gaudy attire. There were many others who were there solely for the play and acting. It is safe to say there was no one present who bore quite the attitude which Mrs. Sommers did to her surroundings. She gathered in the whole stage and players and people in one wide impression, and absorbed it and enjoyed it. She laughed at the comedy and wept — she and the gaudy woman next to her wept over the tragedy. And they talked a little together over it. And the gaudy woman wiped her eyes and sniffled on a tiny square of filmy, perfumed lace and passed little Mrs. Sommers her box of candy.

10   The play was over, the music ceased, the crowd filed out. It was like a dream ended. People scattered in all directions. Mrs. Sommers went to the corner and waited for the cable car.

11   A man with keen eyes, who sat opposite to her, seemed to like the study of her small, pale face. It puzzled him to decipher what he saw there. In truth, he saw nothing — unless he were wizard enough to detect a poignant wish, a powerful longing that the cable car would never stop anywhere, but go on and on with her forever.

(817 words)

Reading Comprehension

I. Answer the following questions with the information you read from the passage.

1. What feelings did Mrs. Sommers have after she bought the stockings and boots and well-fitted gloves?
2. Why did Mrs. Sommers enter the restaurant this time rather than go home when she was hungry?
3. Since Mrs. Sommers had a tight purse, why did she leave the waiter a tip at the restaurant as the wealthy people did?
4. Why did the author say, "The play was over, the music ceased, the crowd filed out. It was like a dream ended."?
5. Why did Mrs. Sommers have a poignant wish that the cable car would never stop anywhere, but go on and on with her forever?

II. Topics for discussion and reflection.

1. Those who love shopping may have a lot of money to spend; they take delight in shopping, having a sense of accomplishment afterwards. In other cases, when people are in low spirits, they tend to do more shopping. Discuss with your partners about various shopping psychologies.
2. Some say shopping is cheaper than seeing a psychiatrist. Through shopping, people can find a new focus and achieve a sense of satisfaction. What people cannot solve in real life can be solved through retail therapy. How far do you agree with this opinion?

Exercises for Integrated Skills

I. Dictation

　　Listen to the following passage. Altogether the passage will be read to you four times. During the first reading, which will be read at normal speed, listen and try to understand the meaning. For the second and third readings, the passage will be read sentence by sentence, or phrase by phrase, with *intervals of 15 to 20 seconds. The last reading will be done at normal speed again and during this time you should check your work. You will then be given 2 minutes to check through your work once more.*

II. Cloze

Fill in each blank in the passage below with a word or phrase taken from the box in its appropriate form.

alleviate	depress	control	constant	characteristic
outrage	obsess	suffer	bear	couple with
treat	addict	dog	euphoria	detrimental
drag	dissipate	enjoy	debt	associate with

Shopping can be a __1__ for some and fun for others but for someone who __2__ to shopping it is neither. The compulsive shopper experiences all the general symptoms __3__ addiction.

For people who shop for the "high", shopping makes them suffer from __4__ thoughts about spending when they are not actually acting it out. Their failure to control their spending impacts __5__ on all other aspects of their lives.

Compulsive shoppers believe that shopping will make them feel better. They often shop when they feel __6__, lonely, bored or angry. Shopping offers a palliative for their __7__. While they are spending they experience the kind of __8__ that is similar to the "high" induced by drugs.

While they are on this "high" they tend to spend __9__ amounts of money on things that they don't need. Their closets are full of items still __10__ their tags. The "high" comes with the spending, not with the __11__ of what is purchased.

Because they lose their ability to buy within their means they are ___12___ in financial trouble and often ___13___ by collection agencies. When the "high" of shopping ___14___ they are left with the guilt and shame so ___15___ of the addiction cycle. The guilt and shame may contain the urge for a short while but ultimately it leads to the need to ___16___ the bad feelings through another bout of spending.

Relationships, jobs and financial obligations suffer as the ___17___ spending leads the addict deeper and deeper into ___18___.

There are a number of established organizations that provide help and support for those struggling with a shopping addiction. Compulsive spending is often ___19___ other addictive behaviors so working with the right kind of professional help along with the support of a self-help group is the most effective ___20___.

Oral Activities

Activity One: Q & A

1. Are you a shopping addict? Do you always follow fashion when going shopping?
2. Do you think the items people shop for define who they are?

Activity Two: Work in groups and discuss the following questions.

1. In many women's lives, shopping is a hobby and a must. Some people think women enjoy shopping because they love a bargain. Some hold the opinion that women love to shop because it is the only area of the world where they feel like they are actually in control, while others argue that women shop just for the sheer pleasure of it. Why do most women love to shop from your perspective?
2. Working women have emerged as a potential force in the marketplace and therefore, have become the new target group for marketers. How is rising female consumer power changing the way companies design and sell their products? What have companies done to attract female consumers? Share what you have observed with your classmates.

Unit 7 Shopping

Activity Three: Shopping Guide

Find some students in the class who are "shopping experts". Ask them to act as shopping guides for other students—consumers who want to know some information, e.g., skills or strategies in shopping.

Now work in groups to act out a play. You can talk about shopping strategies to stretch your dollar, different shopping experiences, or some good places to shop for certain items.

Writing Practice

Note Writing: Replying to Inquiries

Your friend Lisa plans to go to Hong Kong/Beijing/Shanghai/your hometown to do some shopping. She asks you for some good shopping places and tips. Write a note to reply to her inquiries.

```
                                              23 ____,  _____
Dear Lisa,



                                                      Yours,
                                                      _____
```

Composition Writing

Shopping via internet, SMS (cellphone) or TV has changed the way people make purchases. Have you experienced any new ways of shopping mentioned above? Write a composition in about 120 words to compare the advantages and disadvantages of traditional shopping and new ways of shopping.

Unit 8 Women around the World

Warm-up Activities

1. Divide the class into groups and discuss what makes an "ideal" woman from the perspectives of personality, physical appearance, education and family background, job, and personal value and belief.
2. Different cultures impose different expectations upon women. What roles do you think a woman should play in the family and society today in the Chinese society?

Text I

The Feminine Mystique

Pre-reading Questions

1. What social roles are traditionally expected for Chinese women?
2. Do you think the fulfillment of biological and social roles will make women perfect and complete?

1   The problem lay buried, unspoken, for many years in the minds of American women. It was a strange stirring, a sense of dissatisfaction, a yearning that women suffered in the middle of the twentieth century in the United States. Each suburban wife struggled with it alone. As she made the beds, shopped for groceries, matched slipcover material, ate peanut butter sandwiches with her

children, chauffeured Cub Scouts and Brownies, lay beside her husband at night —she was afraid to ask even of herself the silent question —"Is this all?"

2   For over fifteen years there was no word of this yearning in the millions of words written about women, for women, in all the columns, books and articles by experts telling women their role was to seek fulfillment as wives and mothers. Over and over women heard in voices of tradition and of Freudian sophistication that they could desire no greater destiny than to glory in their own femininity. Experts told them how to catch a man and keep him, how to breastfeed children and handle their toilet training, how to cope with sibling rivalry and adolescent rebellion; how to buy a dishwasher, bake bread, cook gourmet snails, and build a swimming pool with their own hands; how to dress, look, and act more feminine and make marriage more exciting; how to keep their husbands from dying young and their sons from growing into delinquents.

3   In the fifteen years after World War II, this mystique of feminine fulfillment became the cherished and self-perpetuating core of contemporary American culture. Millions of women lived their lives in the image of those pretty pictures of the American suburban housewife, kissing their husbands goodbye in front of the picture window, depositing their children at school, and smiling as they ran the new electric waxer over the spotless kitchen floor. They baked their own bread and sewed their own and their children's clothes, kept their new washing machines and dryers running all day. They changed the sheets on the beds twice a week instead of once, took the rug-hooking class in adult education, and pitied their poor frustrated mothers, who had dreamed of having a career. Their only dream was to be perfect wives and mothers; their highest ambition to have five children and a beautiful house; their only fight to get and keep their husbands. They had no thought for the unfeminine problems of the world outside the home; they wanted the men to make the major decisions. They gloried in their role as women, and wrote proudly on the census blank: "Occupation: housewife."...

4   But on an April morning in 1959, I heard a mother of four having coffee with four other mothers in a suburban development fifteen miles from New York, say in a tone of quiet desperation, "the problem." And the others knew, without words, that she was not talking about a problem with her husband, or her children, or her home. Suddenly they all realized they shared the same problem, the problem that has no name...

5   If I am right, the problem that has no name stirring in the minds of so many American women today is not a matter of loss of femininity or too much education, or the demands of domesticity. It is far more important than anyone recognizes. It is the key to these other new and old problems which have been torturing women and their husbands and children, and puzzling their doctors and educators for years. It may well be the key to our future as a nation and a culture. "I want something more than my husband and my children and my home."...

6   Then the split in the image will be healed, and daughters will not face that jumping-off point at twenty-one or forty-one. When their mothers' fulfillment makes girls sure they want to be women, they will not have to "beat themselves down" to be feminine; they can stretch and stretch until their own efforts will tell them who they are. They will not need the regard of boy or man to feel alive. And when women do not need to live through their husbands and children, men will not fear the love and strength of women, nor need another's weakness to prove their own masculinity. They can finally see each other as they are. And this may be the next step in human evolution.

7   Who knows what women can be when they are finally free to become themselves? Who knows what women's intelligence will contribute when it can be nourished without denying love? Who knows of the possibilities of love when men and women share not only children, home, and garden, not only the fulfillment of their biological roles, but the responsibilities and passions of the work that creates the human future and the full human knowledge of who they are? It has barely begun, the search of women for themselves. But the time is at hand when the voices of the feminine mystique can no longer drown out the inner voice that is driving women on to becoming complete.

(845 words)

Unit 8 Women around the World

Words and Expressions

mystique	/mɪˈstiːk/	n.	a quality that makes someone or something seem mysterious, exciting, or special 神秘气氛,神秘性
stirring	/ˈstɜːrɪŋ/	n.	an early sign that something is starting to happen, or that you are beginning to feel a particular emotion（某事或某种情感的）先兆
yearning	/ˈjɜːnɪŋ/	n.	a strong desire for something 向往,思慕
suburban	/səˈbɜːbən/	adj.	related to a suburb, or in a suburb 郊区的,城郊的
slipcover	/ˈslɪpˌkʌvə/	n.	a loose cloth cover for furniture 家具套
peanut butter			a spread for bread made of crushed peanuts 花生酱
chauffeur	/ˈʃəʊfə/	vt.	to drive someone in your car, especially when you do not want to（尤指非情愿地）开车带……到处转
Cub Scout			幼年童子军成员
Brownies			幼年女童子军成员
fulfillment	/fʊlˈfɪlmənt/	n.	(fulfilment BrE) the feeling of being happy and satisfied with your life because you are doing interesting, useful, or important things 满足感
Freudian	/ˈfrɔɪdɪən/	adj.	relating to Sigmund Freud's ideas about the way the mind works, and the way it can be studied 弗洛伊德学说的
sophistication	/səˌfɪstɪˈkeɪʃən/	n.	the quality of being intelligent and knowing a lot, so that you are able to understand complicated situations 老练,老于世故
destiny	/ˈdestɪnɪ/	n.	the things that will happen to someone in the future, especially those that cannot be changed or controlled 命运,天命
glory	/ˈglɔːrɪ/	vi.	(to glory in sth.) to enjoy or be proud of something 以……自豪,高兴
bake	/beɪk/	vt.	to cook something using dry heat, in an oven 烤,焙,烘

cherish	/ˈtʃerɪʃ/	vt.	if you cherish something, it is very important to you 珍视，维护 **cherished** *adj.* 被珍视的，重要的
perpetuate	/pəˈpetʃueɪt/	vt.	to make a situation, attitude, etc., especially a bad one, continue to exist for a long time 使（不好的情形、制度、信仰等）继续，延长 **self-perpetuating** *adj.* 自我延续的
picture window			a large window made of a single piece of glass that provides a broad outside view 大型落地窗，观景窗
deposit	/dɪˈpɒzɪt/	vt.	to put someone or something down in a particular place 放下，放置
waxer	/ˈwæksə/	n.	a machine used to rub a layer of wax into a floor, surface, etc. to protect it or make it shine 打蜡机
spotless	/ˈspɒtləs/	adj.	completely clean 极其清洁的，一尘不染的
dryer	/ˈdraɪə/	n.	a machine that dries things, especially clothes 烘干机；干燥机；脱水机
rug	/rʌg/	n.	a piece of thick cloth or wool that covers part of a floor, used for warmth or as a decoration 小地毯，垫子
frustrated	/frʌˈstreɪtɪd/	adj.	feeling annoyed, upset, and impatient, because you cannot control or change a situation, or achieve something 沮丧的，懊恼的
census	/ˈsensəs/	n.	an official process of counting a country's population and finding out about the people 人口普查
desperation	/ˌdespəˈreɪʃən/	n.	the feeling that you have when you are in such a bad situation that you will try anything to change it 绝望，孤注一掷
stir	/stɜː/	vi.	if a feeling stirs in you, you begin to feel it (感情、情绪) 产生，萌动
femininity	/ˌfemɪˈnɪnɪtɪ/	n.	qualities that are considered to be typical of women, especially qualities that are gentle, delicate, and pretty 女性气质，女性特质
domesticity	/ˌdəʊmeˈstɪsɪtɪ/	n.	life at home with your family 家庭生活

Unit 8 Women around the World

torture	/ˈtɔːtʃə/	vt.	to cause intense suffering to 折磨, 使难受
split	/splɪt/	n.	a clear separation or difference between two things 分化, 区分
jumping-off point			a place to start from, especially at the beginning of a journey 起点, 出发点
beat someone down			to make someone feel defeated, so they no longer respect themselves 打压, 使沮丧
stretch	/stretʃ/	vi.	to make something bigger or looser by pulling it, or to become bigger or looser as a result of being pulled 延伸
masculinity	/ˌmæskjʊˈlɪnɪtɪ/	n.	qualities that are considered to be typical of men 男子气概, 阳刚之气
nourish	/ˈnʌrɪʃ/	vt.	to keep a feeling, idea, or belief strong or help it to grow stronger 增进, 助长
deny	/dɪˈnaɪ/	vt.	to refuse to allow someone to have or do something 拒绝给予, 不允许（某人拥有某物）
passion	/ˈpæʃən/	n.	a very strong feeling about something or a strong belief in something 热情, 激情
at hand			likely to happen soon 即将到来
drown	/draʊn/	vt.	(also drown out) to prevent a sound from being heard 盖过, 淹没 (声音)
inner	/ˈɪnə/	adj.	inner thoughts or feelings are ones that you feel strongly but do not always show to other people 内心的

Reading Comprehension

I. **Summarize the paragraphs into a few sentences, which indicate the main idea of the article.**

Para. 1 _____

_____

Para. 2 _____
       _____

Para. 3 _____
       _____

Para. 4 _____
       _____

Para. 5 _____
       _____

II. **Fill in the blanks to complete the summary of the text.**

In the wake of World War II, women were made to believe that their self-fulfillment could only be found in _____. The women of the 1950s were molded for "occupation housewife". They were victims of a false belief system that requires them to find identity and meaning in their lives through _____. The author defined women's unhappiness as "the problem that has no name" which was a longing for _____. She puts the blame on an idealized image of femininity that she calls the feminine mystique. According to the author, women were encouraged to confine themselves to the narrow roles of _____ _____, forsaking education and career aspirations in the process. The author made an attempt to prove that _____, which can ultimately lead to problems for women and their families. Women's fulfillment not only lies in _____, but also in _____ _____.

III. **Answer the following questions.**

1. What is the author's purpose in writing this article?
2. What does "this mystique of feminine fulfillment" (Para. 3) refer to?
3. What is the problem that has no name? Does the author give an answer in the end?
4. What does "jumping-off point at twenty-one or forty-one" (Para. 6) mean?
5. What can be inferred from the last sentence of the passage? What was the author's attitude towards the future of women?

Unit 8   Women around the World

IV. Paraphrase the following sentences within the context.

1. (Para. 3) In the fifteen years after World War II, this mystique of feminine fulfillment became the cherished and self-perpetuating core of contemporary American culture.

2. (Para. 3) They gloried in their role as women, and wrote proudly on the census blank: "Occupation: housewife."

3. (Para. 6) Then the split in the image will be healed, and daughters will not face that jumping-off point at twenty-one or forty-one.

4. (Para. 6) And when women do not need to live through their husbands and children, men will not fear the love and strength of women, nor need another's weakness to prove their own masculinity.

5. (Para. 7) Who knows of the possibilities of love when men and women share not only children, home and garden, not only the fulfillment of their biological roles, but the responsibilities and passions of the work that creates the human future and the full human knowledge of who they are?

6. (Para. 7) But the time is at hand when the voices of the feminine mystique can no longer drown out the inner voice that is driving women on to becoming complete.

Vocabulary Exercises

I. Fill in each blank with one of the following words from each pair and note the difference of meaning between them. Change the form when necessary.

1. MYSTIQUE   MYSTERY

   a. Some of the _____ surrounding the basketball player has gone forever.

   b. How life began on Earth is one of the great _____ of science.

   c. When I was a little boy, many quiet summer nights, I'd lie on my back, looking into the sky dotted with stars and fascinated by the _____ of the remote universe.

   d. The circumstances of his death were still veiled in _____.

   e. Part of the Valley's _____ lies in its secrets.

2. POSSIBILITY   PROBABILITY

   a. The old woman believed that there is always a _____ that her son might go back to her.

   b. Having disappeared for long, the kid has been kidnapped in all _____.

   c. Failure is a _____.

   d. Such accidents are not only _____ but also _____.

   e. According to the weather forecast, there is a remote _____ of snow on high ground tomorrow.

   f. There's a high _____ that the children will follow a different career.

II. Fill in the blank in each sentence with a word or phrase taken from the box in its appropriate form.

perpetuate	deposit	feminine	glory in
beat down	domesticity	masculinity	torture
heal	stir	drown out	a matter of

1. The noise of their battle _____ by the aircraft's engine.
2. These measures will _____ the hostility between the two ethnic groups.

3. The woman _____ her bag directly at the counter.
4. She doesn't like to _____ her past achievements.
5. Unlike the other girls, Amelia's report describes the experience from a(n) _____ point of view.
6. It's generally believed that children's ideas of _____ tend to come from their fathers.
7. Rachel sat alone for hours at home, _____ by jealousy of her sister's beautiful dress.
8. Impressed by such a scene of happy _____, she wants a home very much.
9. The trauma of divorce can usually _____ by a successful remarriage.
10. The incident _____ students to protest against the school regulations.
11. Experiencing a series of setbacks, the woman seemed _____.
12. I simply can't take the money. It's _____ principle.

Translation Exercises

Translate each of the following sentences into English, using the word or phrase given in the brackets.

1. 女儿出国读书前,他珍惜每一个和她在一起的机会,那段时光充满了欢乐。(cherish)

2. 房子着火后,他立刻冲进去救那个被大火包围的孩子,全然不顾自己的安危。(have no thought for)

3. 我们同情所有在地震中失去亲人无家可归的人们。(pity)

4. 杰克的父母希望他能像他父亲一样成为一名出色的外科医生,但他却一直梦想成为一名电台音乐节目主持人。(dream of)

5. 当我们向老板汇报工作时,他总是以命令的口吻说话,这使我们感到紧张和压抑。(in a tone of...)

6. 两国把今天的和平谈判当作新的起点，并承诺在将来不断巩固和发展两国间的友好合作关系。(jumping-off point)

7. 你只有两条路可以选择：要么被痛苦击倒，要么把痛苦踩在脚下。(beat down)

8. 她带着三个孩子挺过了这段艰难的日子，这都源于她的坚强与信念。(live through)

9. 我们本想谈论歌手的演唱风格，可乐队的声音盖过了我们的谈话，我们只好坐着一言不发。(drown out)

Text II

Still a Perfect 10

Pre-reading Question

1. Do you know any world famous women athletes?
2. Do you like watching women's artistic gymnastics? Who are your favorite gymnasts? Why?

1 There have been many remarkable women athletes during the 109-year history of the modern Olympic Movement, but few have had the global impact of the young girl from rural Onesti, Romania, named Nadia Comaneci. Even today, almost 30 years after her greatest triumphs, you need only mention the word "Nadia" and sports fans around the world know instantly to whom you are referring.

2 The 1976 Olympic Games opened in Montreal with some uncertainty hanging over them. Memories of the massacre of 11 Israeli athletes at the 1972 Munich Games still lingered in many people's minds and 26 African nations had boycotted the Montreal Games. With the modern Olympic Games becoming

a global forum to protest geopolitical issues, many sports pundits predicted tough times ahead for the Games.

However, on the first full day of the women's gymnastics competition, everything changed. Nadia Comaneci stepped up to the uneven bars and did something no other Olympic gymnast had ever accomplished. She scored a perfect score of 10. Her perfect score in the Olympic Games, sport's biggest stage, resonated throughout the world. This moment of "perfection" changed gymnastics, the Olympic Games and her life forever. This mark, in fact, was so unexpected that the electronic scoring system could only display the score as a 1.00. Comaneci says, "Even today, not many people remember how many medals I won, but they still remember that first perfect 10."

After scoring seven perfect marks during the course of the competition, Nadia left Montreal with five Olympic medals (three golds, one silver and a bronze) and super stardom. American sports writer Frank DeFord said, "Had she scored a 9.999, nothing would have changed, but the 'Perfect 10' changed everything. Nobody had the foggiest idea who she was or where she had come from, but she became the icon of the Games."

Three months before her 1976 Olympic Games triumph, the American public witnessed a preview of Nadia's expertise when she competed in the 1st American Cup, in Madison Square Garden in New York City. There, she easily won the competition and scored two perfect 10s in the process. Comaneci shared the winner's podium with a young American, Bart Conner, who was celebrating his 18th birthday that very day. Twenty years later, Bart and Nadia would become husband and wife.

From 1976 until 1980, Nadia struggled with the demands of celebrity, puberty and gymnastics. Although during this time she won two of three successive European All-Around titles and four World Championships medals, her personal struggles dominated the media coverage of her.

Nevertheless, Nadia managed to arrive in Moscow for the 1980 Games with completely new exercises and the competitive desire to delight the world again. However, she made a mistake on the uneven bars in the first round of optional exercises, which seemed to eliminate her chances of defending her All-Around Olympic title. After a prolonged judging of her balance beam routine, which took 28 minutes to resolve, Comaneci took home the silver medal behind her Soviet rival, Elena Davydova. By the end of the Games, Comaneci had earned two gold and two silver medals for Romania. The impact of this brilliant performance was reduced, partly because the US-led boycott restricted some countries' television coverage of the Games and partly because nothing could have possibly matched her historic perfection of 1976. Comaneci says, "Many people say to me, 'I guess you didn't do very well in 1980. What happened?' Well, actually, I got two golds and two silvers, I don't think that is too bad."

8   After the 1980 Moscow Games, Nadia was rarely seen outside the Communist bloc of nations. Her last official competition was at the World University Games in 1981 in Bucharest where she won gold medals in every event; nevertheless, Nadia saved her retirement announcement for early 1984. It was at this retirement party that Juan Antonio Samaranch, then President of the IOC, awarded her the Olympic Order for her illustrious career in the sport of gymnastics.

9   Life in Romania under President Nicolae Ceausescu had become increasingly difficult even for the young woman who had put the country on the map. "I was rarely allowed to travel outside of Romania, except to Moscow, and once I went to Cuba," Comaneci recalls. Therefore, it was surprising that she was allowed to attend the 1984 Los Angeles Games as a guest of chief organiser, Peter Ueberroth.

10 Finally, in November 1989, Nadia escaped from her homeland as she crossed the border to Hungary and then on to Austria. After making contact with the US Embassy in Vienna, Comaneci was given political refugee status and she boarded a plane for New York City. It was only three weeks later that the Romanian revolution began. To this day, many Romanians salute Nadia for her willingness to risk her life for freedom. Comaneci eventually made her way to Montreal where she lived with Romanian friends, until September 1991 when she moved to Norman, Oklahoma, to be with her old acquaintance and new boyfriend, Conner. In 1995, Nadia donated USD100,000 to the Romanian Gymnastics Federation to help the gymnastics team prepare for the Atlanta Games.

11 In April 1996, she married Conner, a two-time US Olympic gold medallist, in a lavish state wedding in Bucharest. The Lido Hotel was renamed "Hotel

Nadia" for the month of April and became her residence so that she and Bart could host the more than 100 guests who came to celebrate their union. More than 10,000 Romanians lined the streets of Bucharest to cheer for their legendary heroine on her wedding day. The 20th century ended with Nadia being named in many lists of important contributors to society. In Austria, at the famous Vienna Opera House, she was awarded the World Sports Award of the Century. She also made the list of *People* magazine's "100 Most Important Moments of the Century" and ABC Television and *Ladies' Home Journal*'s "50 Most Significant Moments in Television History".

12 Even 30 years after her greatest sports moment, Nadia continues to be in demand. She recently signed a four-year sponsorship contract that includes annual donations to the Nadia Comaneci School of Gymnastics in Onesti and the Nadia Comaneci Children's Clinic in Bucharest. Although she helps out with many different charities, Nadia remains very active in three in particular. She is the Co-Chairman of the Board of Directors of the Special Olympics International, a Vice-President of the Muscular Dystrophy Association and a founding member of the Laureus Sports Foundation.

13 She travels all over the world to promote the values of sports to disenfranchised children. In 2004, Comaneci was awarded the IOC Olympic Order for the second time. IOC President Jacques Rogge honoured her on this occasion for her continuing work to promote sports, especially gymnastics, all over the world. She says, "I have worked with Nelson Mandela, and I have heard him say, 'sport has the power to change the world,' so I am happy to use my celebrity to help others."

14 Although many wish to freeze Nadia in the one very special moment in time when she made global history by scoring the first perfect 10, she would be the first to say, "I rarely look back at either the good times or the bad ones. I prefer to live in the present, and my present couldn't be more perfect."

(1,218 words)

Reading Comprehension

I. **Answer the following questions with the information you read from the passage.**

1. What happened during the 1972 Munich Games? What impact did it have on the 1976 Olympic Games?
2. What changed Nadia Comaneci's life forever?
3. Why was the impact of Nadia's brilliant performance on the 1980 Games reduced?
4. Why did Nadia escape from her homeland?
5. What awards did Nadia obtain during her life? Why?

II. **Topics for discussion and reflection.**

1. What did Nadia Comaneci imply when she said, "For me personally, life has an essential dimension that makes you feel truly fulfilled: human solidarity"?
2. Make a survey of the development of women's sports in the Olympic history. Present your findings to the class with examples.

Exercises for Integrated Skills

I. **Dictation**

Listen to the following passage. Altogether the passage will be read to you four times. During the first reading, which will be read at normal speed, listen and try to understand the meaning. For the second and third readings, the passage will be read sentence by sentence, or phrase by phrase, with intervals of 15 to 20 seconds. The last reading will be done at normal speed again and during this time you should check your work. You will then be given 2 minutes to check through your work once more.

Unit 8 Women around the World

II. Cloze

Fill in each blank in the passage below with a word or phrase taken from the box in its appropriate form.

appear	nature	inferior	conclude	equal
dominant	respect	splash	mug	light
responsible	insult	historical	challenge	protect

For a long period before the 1960s, women were considered to be the weaker sex, just as Shakespeare said in Hamlet:

"Frailty, thy name is woman."

In contrast, men were regarded as the stronger and the ___1___ sex. In this light men should undertake the duty to adopt a ___2___ attitude toward the so-called weaker sex.

This implied that men should help women on and off with their coats, ___3___ their cigarettes, open the doors for them to get on and off the wagon, train, bus, etc. or to enter houses. Have you ever seen the movie "Titanic"? Well, when the ship was sinking, it was the women who had the right to get on the lifeboats first, just because men had the ___4___ for taking care of and protecting women!

This could lead to the ___5___ that the custom "Lady First" was developed out of respect in ___6___, but in fact it was kind of looking down upon women in ___7___.

In the 1960s, women began to ___8___ this tradition. As one lady put it, "___9___, men should walk on the outside of the pavement so as to prevent the lady's dress from being spoilt by mud ___10___ by a carriage. Today a man is supposed to walk on the outside. A man should walk where he wants to. So should a woman. If out of love and ___11___, he actually wants to take the blows, he should walk on the inside, because that's where ___12___ are hiding these days."

This shows that to treat a woman as ___13___ just because she is a female is not only ___14___ but also out of step with contemporary American culture.

Women may go to the restaurants Dutch treat. They may refuse such words as chairman, businessman, policeman... Instead they prefer chairperson, busi nessperson, police or cop...just to show that they are ___15___ in every respect with male!

Oral Activities

Women's Roles in the Past, at Present, and in the Future

Women's roles have changed a lot due to women's liberation. However, there still exist prejudices and bias against women in the world. In many countries, women are not treated equally to men in terms of voting right, salary, etc., and are still fighting for their future.

Now work in groups to stage a performance about women's roles in the past, at present, and in the future based on what you have read or heard of. You can focus on women's status at home, at work, or in social activities.

Writing Practice

Notice Writing: An Notice

Write a notice to all of the students in the English Department, notifying them of Betty Author's book signing ceremony which will be held at the school auditorium next Friday.

25 ____, 20____

Dear students,

Sincerely yours,
The Students' Union

Composition Writing

Write a composition about a woman whom you admire in about 120 words, using the outcome of oral activities. Emphasis should be laid on her various qualities that you admire so much.

Unit 9 Travel

Warm-up Activities

Holiday Itinerary

Step One: Imagine you are a tour guide and have been asked to make an itinerary for a tourist group. Work in groups to create the itinerary, listing the places of interest and scenic spots you think are worth visiting and explain your reasons briefly. Below is some information about two different groups. You can choose either one.

Group 1: A group of young Americans who plan to travel in China for two weeks

Group 2: A group of young Chinese who plan to visit Europe / North America

Step Two: Offer some travel tips to these young tourists who have never been to China or Europe / North America before.

Text I

Transformative Travel

Pre-reading Questions

1. Why do people travel?
2. Have you ever tried to make any changes to your life? How did you do that?

Unit 9 Travel

1   Many people are not interested in changing themselves. They already like things the way they are or they aren't prepared to make significant changes in their lives. Such changes need not include quitting your job, getting a divorce, or moving to the South Pacific. Transformative changes do not necessarily alter what you do on the outside, but they can produce dramatic alterations in your outlook and new responses to different situations. 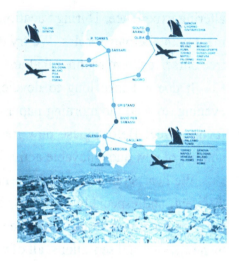 Much depends on what you are missing, what you are searching for, and what you would like to do differently.

2   The object of transformative travel ought to be the kind of growth that helps you bring home and make part of you, forever, whatever you learned about yourself while you were gone. These changes can make your daily life a holiday in the sense that you derive great pleasure from experiences you now take for granted. You can learn about such changes in therapy or from a book. You learn it better and quicker, however, when you find yourself in novel situations that force you to develop new resources and respond creatively to challenges you face.

3   Travel may be more effective than therapy for people who need to make changes in their lives. It is a way to create a new future for oneself.

4   Gully Wells, a travel writer, describes travel as a kind of drug, an altered state of consciousness in which you are transported not only to another place, but to another dimension. Your hearing and vision are hypersensitive, every smell and sensation becomes more intense. There is no other human activity that has greater potential to alter your perceptions or the way you choose your life.

5   The truth is that most people are bored with aspects of their lives. We frequent the same restaurants, endure the same rush-hour traffic, and follow predictable routines in our social lives. Our days are rigidly structured, more so than we ever realize.

6   While our daily routines and familiar patterns are comforting to a certain degree, even enjoyable in their familiar pleasures, they also make us feel deprived of stimulation. That is where the magic of travel comes in as a life-

altering experience. During vacations, we move at a different pace. We experiment with alternative roles. We try different foods, engage in unusual activities, free ourselves from routines that are most familiar.

7   It doesn't take long to develop new repetitive patterns—to stroll in the evening, to read the morning paper on the balcony, to lie on the beach under a favorite tree. Before these new routines become boring, we have tried out a number of new and enjoyable activities.

8   We hear strange accents and novel sounds in the streets. The food tastes different, and especially the smells all around us cry out for our attention. We see people acting in strange and often incomprehensible ways. We are bombarded
9   by new sights and sensations, all of which act to transport us to another world.

In a study of leisure behavior, French sociologist Joffre Dumazedier described the escape that takes place during travel as a "secondary reality," one in which fantasies may be acted out. The appeal of cruises and resorts, for instance, is the way they pamper you and let you live in a fantasy world. For a week or two, you can pretend to be part of the leisure class, with nothing better to do than decide what to eat and whether to take a nap, a walk, or go shopping. You pretend you are a millionaire as you sip pina coladas on your private veranda, watching the sunset, or a naturalist as you wander through the woods studying plant life and bird sounds, or a champion surfer as you play on the waves.

10 One of the things that is unique about travel, at least for adults, is that it takes place in a world of fantasy and play. Under such circumstances, you willingly suspend normal boundaries of reality to take on alternative roles of make-believe. In a book on marketing techniques, Edward Mayo and Lance Jarvis remind travel agents that they are essentially selling people's dreams.

11 Campers and backpackers abandon their comfortable homes and modern conveniences in order to venture out in the wilderness and pretend to live off the land. They engage in "symbolic labor"—chopping wood, tracking, fishing, hunting—all reminiscent of our ancestral past. In a sense, they pretend they are living in the past for a while when they isolate themselves in this way. Behavior tends to regress to a more basic level, and conversations take on a more raucous, uninhibited flavor. A wilderness excursion is a game of make-believe in which the participants use travel to change their usual environment dramatically, a

process that creates unique conditions likely to produce novel, memorable experiences.

12   The change of scenery that traveling provides is often just the antidote you need during times when life seems to be unraveling around you.

13   A woman whose husband had recently died found herself losing all sense of reality: "My life with my husband had started to feel like it had been a dream," she said. "Had I only imagined it all?" While therapy is often one solution for people struggling to find their way—as are less constructive options like alcohol or withdrawal—this woman decided to use travel as a way to heal herself. Her plan was to revisit some of the places she had once shared with her husband. By reexperiencing old sights and sounds, she was eventually able to resolve some issues she had struggled with.

14   People are motivated not only to confront their fantasies but also to indulge them.

15   Recreational travel is ordinarily conceived of as a form of leisure activity, along with passive diversions, such as watching television and spectator sports, and activities such as gardening and hobbies. People say such activities help them to relax, to escape from routines, and allow them the freedom to do whatever they want.

16   Travel also provides "time outs" from usual responsibilities and supplies a degree of stimulation and excitement that could not be possible otherwise. It is therefore unusual to think about using travel to promote self-esteem, self-confidence, and well-being in the same sense in which you might consult a psychologist or personal trainer.

17   Taking a trip, even an adventurous, unstructured trip, is no guarantee that you will grow significantly as a result. However, facing each day with a spirit of adventure, encountering people with openness and flexibility, and pushing yourself to do things differently creates personal growth.

18   Travel is not really an escape from normal life, nor is it an insulated reality. Travel is a reminder of what is possible for you to experience every waking moment of your life.

(1,129 words)

Words and Expressions

therapy	/ˈθerəpɪ/	n.	the treatment of an illness or injury over a fairly long period of time 疗法
novel	/ˈnɒvəl/	adj.	new and original, not like anything seen before 新奇的, 新颖的
alter	/ˈɔːltə/	vi./vt.	to change (使)变化
vision	/ˈvɪʒən/	n.	the ability to see 视力
hypersensitive	/ˌhaɪpəˈsensɪtɪv/	adj.	very easily influenced, changed or damaged 过敏的
potential	/pəˈtenʃəl/	n.	the possibility to develop, achieve, or succeed 可能性, 潜在性
perception	/pəˈsepʃən/	n.	the way of seeing or understanding something 认识, 看法
frequent	/ˈfriːkwənt/	vt.	to go to a particular place often 常去(某地方)
endure	/ɪnˈdjʊə/	vt.	to suffer something difficult, unpleasant or painful 忍耐, 容忍
structure	/ˈstrʌktʃə/	vt.	to plan or organize 组织, 安排
comforting	/ˈkʌmfətɪŋ/	adj.	making you feel less worried, unhappy, or upset 令人感到安慰的
deprive	/dɪˈpraɪv/	vt.	to take something, especially something necessary or pleasant, away from someone 剥夺
magic	/ˈmædʒɪk/	n.	a special, attractive, or exciting quality 魅力, 魔力
repetitive	/rɪˈpetɪtɪv/	adj.	done many times in the same way, and boring 重复的, 反复的
stroll	/strəʊl/	vi.	to walk somewhere in a slow relaxed way 散步, 漫步
incomprehensible	/ɪnˌkɒmprɪˈhensɪbəl/	adj.	difficult or impossible to understand 不可理解的, 难懂的
bombard	/bɒmˈbɑːd/	vt.	to attack verbally 口头上攻击
sociologist	/ˌsəʊʃɪˈɒlədʒɪst/	n.	someone who studies sociology or is an expert in sociology 社会学家
act out			to express thoughts, emotions or ideas in actions 表现出来

cruise	/kruːz/	n.	a journey by boat for pleasure 乘船巡游
resort	/rɪˈzɔːt/	n.	a place where a lot of people go for holidays 度假胜地
pamper	/ˈpæmpə/	vt.	to treat a person or an animal in a special way by making them as comfortable as possible and giving them whatever they want 过分呵护，娇惯
nap	/næp/	n.	a short sleep, especially during the day（尤指白天的）小睡，打盹
sip	/sɪp/	vi./vt.	to drink something slowly, taking very small mouthfuls 小口地喝
veranda	/vəˈrændə/	n.	an open area with a floor and a roof that is attached to the side of a house at ground level 游廊，走廊
sunset	/ˈsʌnset/	n.	the time of day when the sun disappears and night begins 日落，黄昏
naturalist	/ˈnætʃərəlɪst/	n.	someone who studies plants or animals 博物学家
surfer	/ˈsɜːfə/	n.	someone who rides on waves while standing on a special board 冲浪者
suspend	/səˈspend/	vt.	to stop something temporarily 暂停
camper	/ˈkæmpə/	n.	someone who is staying in a tent or shelter 露营者
backpacker	/ˈbækˈpækə/	n.	someone who is travelling for pleasure, usually without very much money, and who walks or uses public transport and carries a backpack 背包旅行者
venture	/ˈventʃə/	vi.	to go somewhere that could be dangerous 冒险
wilderness	/ˈwɪldənɪs/	n.	a large area of land that has never been developed or farmed 荒野
live off the land			to grow all the food you need 靠土地生活
symbolic	/sɪmˈbɒlɪk/	adj.	important but not having any real effect 象征性的
chop	/tʃɒp/	vt.	to cut something into smaller pieces 砍，劈

reminiscent	/ˌremɪˈnɪsənt/	adj.	reminding you of something 使人想起某事的
regress	/rɪˈgres/	vi.	to go back to an earlier and worse condition, or to a less developed way of behaving 回归，倒退
raucous	/ˈrɔːkəs/	adj.	impolite, noisy, and violent 混乱的，无礼的
uninhibited	/ˌʌnɪnˈhɪbɪtɪd/	adj.	confident or relaxed enough to do or say what you want to 无拘无束的，不受约束的
flavor	/ˈfleɪvə/	n.	a quality or feature that makes something have a particular style or character 情调，特色
excursion	/ɪkˈskɜːʃən/	n.	a short journey usually for pleasure, often with a group of people 短途旅行
participant	/pɑːˈtɪsɪpənt/	n.	someone who is taking part in an activity or event 参加者，参与者
memorable	/ˈmemərəbəl/	adj.	very good, enjoyable, or unusual, and worth remembering 难忘的，值得纪念的
antidote	/ˈæntɪdəʊt/	n.	something that makes an unpleasant situation better 缓解之物
unravel	/ʌnˈrævəl/	vi.	(of a system, plan, organization, etc.) to start to fail 失败，破产
constructive	/kənˈstrʌktɪv/	adj.	useful and helpful, or likely to produce good results 建设性的
option	/ˈɒpʃən/	n.	a choice that you can make in a particular situation 选择
withdrawal	/wɪðˈdrɔːəl/	n.	an act or process of withdrawing; retreat 移开，撤退
motivate	/ˈməʊtɪveɪt/	vt.	to cause someone to behave in a particular way 激励，激发
diversion	/daɪˈvɜːʃən/	n.	an enjoyable activity that you do to stop yourself from becoming bored 消遣，娱乐
spectator sport			观赏竞技运动
self-esteem	/ˌselfɪˈstiːm/	n.	belief and confidence in your own ability and value 自尊心

well-being	/ˌwelˈbiːŋ/	n.	a feeling of being comfortable, healthy, and happy 舒适，健康，幸福
adventurous	/ədˈventʃərəs/	adj.	characterized by unknown dangers and risks 充满危险的
significantly	/sɪɡˈnɪfɪkəntlɪ/	adv.	in an important way or to an important degree 大大地
encounter	/ɪnˈkaʊntə/	vt.	to meet someone without planning to 偶然遇到
insulate	/ˈɪnsjʊleɪt/	vt.	to protect someone or something from outside influences 把（某人）隔离，使隔绝
reminder	/rɪˈmaɪndə/	n.	something that makes you notice, remember, or think about something 让人回想起某事之物

Reading Comprehension

I. Summarize the text into a few sentences, which indicate the main idea of the article.

_____
_____
_____
_____

II. Answer the following questions.

1. How do you understand the title "Transformative Travel"? What is your attitude towards traveling?
2. Why does Gully Wells compare travel to a kind of drug?
3. Do you think that most people are bored with the routines of their lives? Explain your own ideas with specific examples.
4. What do campers and backpackers engage in while venturing out in the wilderness?
5. Why did the woman plan to revisit some of the places she had once shared with her husband?
6. According to the text, what can create personal growth?

III. Judge, according to the text, whether the following statements are true or false. For false statements, write the facts in parentheses.

1. According to Gully Wells, travel has the greatest potential to change your perceptions or the way you choose your life.
   (   )

2. The only unique thing about travel is that it takes place in a world of fantasy and play.
   (   )

3. Most people are bored with the same routines in their social lives.
   (   )

4. A member of the leisure class has nothing better to do than decide what to eat and whether to take a nap, a walk, or go shopping.
   (   )

5. Participants of a wilderness excursion use travel to change their usual environment slightly.
   (   )

6. It is widely accepted that people use travel to promote self-esteem, self-confidence, and well-being.
   (   )

7. Taking a trip guarantees significant personal growth.
   (   )

IV. Paraphrase the following sentences within the context.

1. (Para. 4) Gully Wells, a travel writer, describes travel as a kind of drug, an altered state of consciousness in which you are transported not only to another place, but to another dimension.

2. (Para. 5) We frequent the same restaurants, endure the same rush-hour traffic, and follow predictable routines in our social lives.

3. (Para. 9) The appeal of cruises and resorts, for instance, is the way they

pamper you and let you live in a fantasy world.

4. (Para. 10) Under such circumstances, you willingly suspend normal boundaries of reality to take on alternative roles of make-believe.

5. (Para. 13) While therapy is often one solution for people struggling to find their way—as are less constructive options like alcohol or withdrawal—this woman decided to use travel as a way to heal herself.

6. (Para. 15) Recreational travel is ordinarily conceived of as a form of leisure activity, along with passive diversions, such as watching television and spectator sports, and activities such as gardening and hobbies.

7. (Para. 16) Travel also provides "time outs" from usual responsibilities and supplies a degree of stimulation and excitement that could not be possible otherwise.

Vocabulary Exercises

I. Fill in each blank with one of the following words from each pair and note the difference of meaning between them. Change the form when necessary.

1. INCOMPREHENSIBLE   INCOMPREHENSIVE
   a. His accent made his speech _____ to me.
   b. This brochure provides a _____ guide to British hotels and restaurants.
   c. The review of the case is rather _____.

d. The procedure must be clear and _____ to all staff.

2. CONCEIVE   PERCEIVE

   a. Language may be _____ as a process which arises from social interaction.
   b. Children who do badly in school tests often _____ themselves to be failures.
   c. The manager _____ a plan to increase profits.
   d. He _____ that there was no other way out of the crisis.

II. **Choose a word or phrase that best completes each of the following sentences.**

1. _____ from early childhood, he believed the world had been invented for his entertainment.
   A. Entertained   B. Treated   C. Pampered   D. Hampered
2. If a child is _____ of a linguistic environment, he or she will unlikely learn a language successfully later on.
   A. driven   B. deprived   C. derived   D. distressed
3. Mail service will be _____ because of the postal workers' strike.
   A. deprived   B. abridged   C. shrunk   D. suspended
4. Who do you think will _____ the company if the manager is dismissed?
   A. take over   B. take off   C. take in   D. take on
5. Most people in the countryside live _____ the land.
   A. out   B. with   C. in   D. off
6. A/An _____ interview refers to an interview without any set format but the interviewer may have some key questions formulated in advance.
   A. constructive   B. unstructured   C. structured   D. uninhibited
7. The room is _____ against noise with special materials.
   A. isolated   B. separated   C. insulated   D. divided

Translation Exercises

Translate each of the following sentences into English, using the word or phrase given in the brackets.

1. 因特网极大地改变了我们的工作和生活,提高了我们的工作效率,使我们的生活变得更加方便。(alter)

2. 我们在工作中得到的乐趣,通常取决于我们努力奋斗的过程,而不是奋斗的结果。(derive from)

3. 虽然她对家庭生活感到不满和厌倦,但她没有改变现状的勇气与决心。(be bored with)

4. 在1896年首届现代奥运会上,由于当时社会对妇女的偏见,妇女被剥夺了参加奥运会的权利。(deprive of)

5. 据调查,只有百分之十的美国成年人进行有规律的锻炼。缺乏锻炼是美国肥胖症患者迅速增加的原因。(engage in)

6. 你应该给自己一个尝试新事物的机会,也许你的生活会因此变得更加美好。(try out)

7. 失恋后,他陷入了极端的痛苦之中,只能通过看心理医生来消除内心的抑郁。(find one's way)

8. 在西方国家,很多年轻人年满18岁就不再依靠父母了,而是自己课外打工,挣钱交学费。(live off)

Text II

Sport and Tourism to Stimulate Development

> **Pre-reading Questions**
>
> 1. Have you ever watched a sporting event while visiting another city/country? Was this the main reason for your visit?
> 2. How do you understand the relationship between sport and tourism? How can sport and tourism stimulate social development?
> 3. Are there any similarities between sport and tourism? How are tourism and sport inter-related?

1   Both sport and tourism have become integrated components of the global culture of our times—they are two ancient expressions of the human spirit. Since early times people have travelled—not only as nomads seeking new pastures for their animals, but also as explorers—driven by a curiosity to discover new worlds.

2   Travel is deeply rooted in human culture, behaviour and values. Tourism has played a major role in breaking down the borders and barriers of distrust and prejudice between countries and peoples. It has contributed to better understanding, greater tolerance and to world peace in general. The same can be said of sport. Both international tourism and sport have enhanced the process of globalization and contributed to peace and prosperity. Both have inspired many young people to achieve new goals and make their dreams a reality.

3   A society's values are reflected in the way people travel and in the way they play and practise their sport. It is due to the fact that tourism can never be an end in itself but only a servant of humanity that the World Tourism Organization (WTO) General Assembly approved

a Global Code of Ethics for Tourism.

  There are many similarities between sport and tourism, yet also some fundamental differences. Tourism is an experience-oriented activity, while sport is a performance-oriented activity.

  The experience-oriented dimension can best be illustrated by quoting the example of Joseph Pine in his book *The Experience Economy*. The price of coffee on a plantation would be about one cent. Coffee, in this context, is a product. Once it is roasted, sorted, and professionally packed, it becomes a commodity and the price per cup may rise to 25 cents. The same coffee, freshly ground and brewed in a coffee shop, becomes a service and the price could be 100 cents. However, if it is served in New York, London or Paris in a trendy new coffee boutique, it is an experience and the price could be 500 cents. The ambience and style of the shop becomes a theatre and the coffee an experience. Tourism provides people with experiences.

  Sport is a performance-oriented activity. It is by nature competitive, and the rewards for winning and achieving success become progressively greater as the level of competition increases. Leisure sporting activities are a world away from the competitive intensity of high-level professional sport. The elite sports have all become professional with major entertainment value and they are driven financially by the media and the sports equipment industry. The leisure time sports public, as well as amateur sport participants and youth, provide the market for the sports equipment popularized through superstar endorsements. Performance is richly rewarded. The publicity, money and social status enjoyed by successful athletes create a powerful incentive to train with relentless dedication.

  The noble inspiration of performance and excellence in sport can be derailed by the use of performance-enhancing drugs. We must not be blind to the fact that in both sport and tourism there are negative abuses that conflict with the codes and objectives of the WTO and the IOC. Drug abuse in sport and child abuse as well as environmental degradation in tourism, are examples of this. We must continue to work with dedication to reduce, and where possible eliminate these practises.

  The reality is that sport and tourism also reflect the values and lifestyles as well as some of the sub-cultures of the fast changing social structures that characterize our global village. New trends and lifestyles emerge which have a significant impact on tourism and sport.

9   Tourism was traditionally more orientated to the idea of rest, relaxation and finding relief from psychosomatic wear and tear. The need for tourism to provide this therapeutic service remains important in the high-stressed society of today. However, the emphasis has shifted more onto health and quality of life issues. This trend gave rise to the need to include physical and sporting activities in tourism products. The "feel good" or "wellness" factor has become a new growth sector in tourism. People want active holidays where they can enjoy the "good things" (sports, exercising) for which there is no time in their everyday life. This has created a boom in tourism involving sports like cycling, golf, jogging, mountaineering, hiking, etc.

10 The evolution of sport and tourism continues. The young free-style generation of today has taken to a whole range of new adventure-type sports such as skateboarding, snowboarding, amongst others, often referred to as "extreme sports". At the same time the artificial experience-based world of sport, such as "aquaparks" and "skidomes", are sprouting up everywhere. These leisure time sports have grown in popularity and many of them have established themselves and receive regular television coverage. "Extreme sports" involve increasing numbers of young people who are losing interest in traditional or elite sports. The competition between extreme and alternative sport, on the one hand, and elite sports, on the other hand, is also increasing.

11 The constant challenge is to adapt and renew the supply of products and services to meet the changing requirements of new generations. It is a known fact that sports disciplines as well as tourism products are subjected to life cycles. With time they lose their original appeal and importance. Management of the process of renewal and the redesigning of products and services is a field where sport and tourism can exchange valuable experiences. Cooperation in this field will be mutually beneficial.

12 Tourism and sport are inter-related—one renders a service to the other. Major sports events such as the Olympic Games and the World Cups in football and rugby, have become important international tourism attractions. The remarkable success of the recent Olympic Games in Sydney is a good example of the significant tourism impact that such events can have.

13 Likewise the tourism industry has served as an "incubator" for new sport disciplines. Tourism has provided an opportunity for leisure activities to be

popularized. With increased popularity they have developed into formally organized sporting activities. Some even progressed from leisure activities to Olympic disciplines. Beach volleyball and snowboarding are two good examples of this.

14   The exceptional growth of tourism over the last 50 years is one of the most remarkable economic and social phenomena of the 20th century. The number of international arrivals shows an evolution from a mere 25 million in 1950 to around 700 million in 2000, representing an average annual growth rate of more than 7% over a period of the last 50 years—well above the average annual economic growth rate for the same period. Tourism has clearly outperformed all other sectors of the economy and has grown into the most significant economic activity in the world. Here are a few indicators of the size and impact of the tourism industry today. According to WTO statistics, tourism on average contributes about 7% of the world's GDP (4-10% in developed countries and much higher in some of the developing countries and island states). About 8% of the world exports are through international visitors' spending on goods and services. That makes tourism the leading export earner,— ahead of the automotive industry, chemicals, food, computers and fuels, with a generated income of US $ 476 billion in 2000 which is the amount spent by tourists annually.

15   The positive impact of tourism and sport on society and particularly on economic development is often misunderstood or underestimated. One reason for this lack of understanding is the absence of reliable statistics that would reflect the knock-on effects of sport and tourism activities.

16   The WTO has also developed Tourism Satellite Accounts (TSA) which will increasingly become a valuable tool for policy and planning purposes. TSA has the objective of establishing a basic language with common definitions and classifications that will provide a picture of the tourism sector in its totality. The TSA methodology may also find useful application in assessing the contribution which sport makes to economic growth and employment.

(1,326 words)

Reading Comprehension

I. Answer the following questions with the information you read from the passage.

1. What roles do sport and tourism play in human culture, behaviour and values?
2. Why is tourism an experience-oriented activity while sport a performance-oriented activity?
3. What has created a boom in tourism involving sports?
4. Why is the impact of tourism and sport on economic development often misunderstood or underestimated?
5. What common interests do sport and tourism share?

II. Topics for discussion and reflection.

1. What is the relationship between sport tour and the other aspects of a trip?
2. Sport tourism involves people travelling to participate in or to observe sports. Currently, sport tourism has become one of the fastest growing sectors of the global travel and tourism industry. What impacts have been brought by the increasing popularity of sport tourism?

Exercises for Integrated Skills

I. Dictation

Listen to the following passage. Altogether the passage will be read to you four times. During the first reading, which will be read at normal speed, listen and try to understand the meaning. For the second and third readings, the passage will be read sentence by sentence, or phrase by phrase, with intervals of 15 to 20 seconds. The last reading will be done at normal speed again and during this time you should check your work. You will then be given 2 minutes to check through your work once more.

Unit 9 Travel

II. Cloze

Fill in each blank in the passage below with a word or phrase taken from the box in its appropriate form.

on-board	among	aggravate	stress	consist of
survey	support	counter	incessant	accumulate
nonprofit	contrary	controlled	bring out	unfortunate
bother	celebrate	negative	respond	experience

　　This is the season of merriment, unless you're traveling next to a loud talker or an ___1___ cell-phone chatterer, says a new Travelocity poll on the state of rude behavior amongst travelers. This ___2___ of more than 1,000 travelers was conceived by Public Agenda, a ___3___ public opinion research organization which conducted a major national study of rudeness in America that was ___4___ by the Pew Charitable Trusts.

　　The study shows that one of the most festive and ___5___ seasons of the year, the winter holiday, can ___6___ some not-so-merry behavior in travelers. While 35 percent of travelers don't think rudeness is a serious issue, the majority of travelers think it can be. However, most travelers (60 percent) are able to shrug rudeness off within a few minutes. With this survey in mind, Travelocity is sharing ways to make the holiday journey a merrier ___7___ through education and some helpful hints.

　　___8___, travel is always considered stressful by many (29 percent), while the survey showed that an equally large group (28 percent) feels that travel during the holidays is the most ___9___ travel time of the year, even above business trips and summer vacations. Airports around the country work to ___10___ this anxiety by offering special holiday programs, such as local musicians and gift-givers for kids. Major airports such as LaGuardia, Chicago Midway, Atlanta, and Dallas/Fort Worth are ___11___ them.

　　According to the survey, one third of ___12___ feel rude travelers and travel personnel are the factors that most ___13___ impact their trip. "___14___ to popular opinion, our study shows that travel is more of a stressor during holiday time than spending time with relatives," said Travelocity editor-at-large, Amy Ziff. "Compare a 28 percent response rate for those who say travel is the most stressful to the 10 percent who cited family."

What bothers people most? It isn't the much talked about food ___15___, although respondents do find fish, ethnic food, items with garlic and fast food to be amongst the most ___16___ items brought on board. Instead, respondents vote that ___17___ children as well as fellow passengers who kick the seat-back in front of them are the most ___18___.

The survey results were ___19___ in Nov. 2003 and ___20___ responses from more than 1,000 Travelocity members.

Oral Activities

Activity One: Adventurous Travel

What should tourists do before travelling? What problems will they possibly come across on their journey? Talk about an adventurous travel based on your own experience.

Activity Two: Work in groups and discuss the following questions.

1. What do you think is the best way to travel? Compare the differences between traveling on a package tour with some friends, and on your own.
2. How might environmental issues affect tourism? What other factors may impact the development of tourism, for instance, global warming, pollution?

Activity Three: Positive and Negative Impacts of Tourism

Tourism can boost economy and help increase the living standard of the local people. However over-reliance on tourism carries significant risks to the local economies, culture, and environment.

Work in groups to make a list of the positive and negative impacts of tourism. Then choose a place with beautiful sceneries and debate about its future development. Should the place be kept natural or should it be fully developed for tourism? Support your ideas with specific details such as figure reports, development plans, visions, etc.

Unit 9   Travel

Writing Practice

Note Writing: Note of Requests

You are going to take a one-week trip to Hangzhou where your close friend Sue lives. Write a note to tell her your travel plan and ask if you can stay in her house for the week.

*28 June, 20*____

Dear Sue,

Yours,

Composition Writing

Most people enjoy travelling as it can be relaxing, interesting, educational, adventurous, etc. Nowadays people are not only touring the famous sightseeing spots, but also exploring some places untravelled before, such as the Antarctic Ocean, and even outer space. Write a composition in about 120 words to state your opinion about these unconventional travel destinations, explaining your viewpoint with supporting details.

Unit 10 Famous People

Warm-up Activities

1. Who am I?
   You are now a famous figure whose name is tagged on your back. But you do not know who you are. Go around the classroom, asking your classmates true / false questions to discover your identity.
2. What, if any, are the negative aspects of being famous? Why do you think so?

Text I

Jefferson Today

Pre-reading Questions

1. How much do you know about Thomas Jefferson and his ideas? Have you ever heard any story about him?
2. What do democracy and freedom mean to you? Does absolute democracy or freedom exist?

1   Thomas Jefferson, who died in 1826, looms ever larger as a figure of special significance. Americans, of course, are familiar with Jefferson as an early statesman, author of the *Declaration of Independence*, and a high-ranking presidential Founding Father. But there is another Jefferson less well known. This is the Jefferson who, as the outstanding American philosopher of democracy,

has an increasing appeal to the world's newly emerging peoples.

2   There is no other man in history who formulated the ideas of democracy with such fullness, persuasiveness, and logic. Those interested in democracy as a political philosophy and system—even those who do not accept his postulates or are critical of his solutions—must reckon with his thought.

3   What, then, is his thought, and how much of it is still relevant under modern conditions?

4   Of all the ideas and beliefs that make up the political philosophy known as Jeffersonian democracy, perhaps three are paramount. These are the idea of equality, the idea of freedom, and the idea of the people's control over government. Underlying the whole, and serving as a major premise, is confidence in man.

5   To Jefferson, it was virtually evident that the human being was essentially good, that he was capable of constant improvement through education and reason. He believed that "no definite limit could be assigned" to man's continued progress from ignorance and superstition to enlightenment and happiness. Unless this is kept in mind, Jefferson can not be understood properly.

6   What did he mean by the concept of equality, which he stated as a "self-evident" truth? Obviously, he was not foolish enough to believe that all men are equal in size or intelligence or talents or moral development. He never said that men are equal, but only that they come into the world with "equal rights". He believed that equality was a political rather than a biological or psychological or economic conception. It was a gift that man acquired automatically by coming into the world as a member of the human community.

7   Intertwined with equality was the concept of freedom, also viewed by Jefferson as a "natural right". In the *Declaration of Independence* he stated it as "self-evident" that liberty was one of the "inherent" and unalienable rights" with which the Creator endowed man. "Freedom", he summed up at one time, "is the gift of Nature."

8   What did Jefferson mean by freedom and why was it necessary for him to claim it as an "inherent" or "natural" right? In Jeffersonian thought there are

two main elements in the idea of freedom. There is, first, man's liberty to organize his own political institutions and to select periodically the individuals to run them. This is political freedom. The other freedom is personal. Foremost in the area of individual liberty, Jefferson believed, was the untrammeled right to say, think, write, and believe whatever the citizen wishes—provided, of course, he does not directly injure his neighbors.

9   It is because political and personal freedom are potentially in conflict that Jefferson, in order to make both secure, felt the need to found them on "natural right". If each liberty derives from an "inherent" right, then neither could justly undermine the other. Experience of the past, when governments were either too strong for the ruled or too weak to rule them, convinced Jefferson of the desirability of establishing a delicate natural balance between political power and personal rights.

10   This brings us to the third basic element in the Jeffersonian idea: the people's control over government. It is paradoxical that Jefferson, who spent most of his adult years in politics, had an ingrained distrust of government as such. For the then-existing governments of Europe, virtually all of them hereditary monarchies, he had antipathy mixed with contempt.

11   Government being a necessity for civilized existence, the question was how it could be prevented from following its tendency to swallow the rights of the people. Jefferson's answer to this ancient dilemma was at variance with much traditional thinking. He began with the postulate that government existed for the people, and not vice versa; that it had no independent being except as an instrument of the people; and that it had no legitimate justification for existence except to serve the people.

12   From this it followed, in Jefferson's view, that only the people, and not their rulers or the privileged classes, could and should be relied upon as the "safe depositories" of political liberty. This key idea in the Jeffersonian political universe rested on the monumental assumption that the people at large had the wisdom, the capability, and the knowledge exclusively to carry the burden of political power and responsibility. The assumption was, of course, widely challenged and vigorously denied in Jefferson's day, but he always asserted his confidence in it.

13   Confidence in the people, however, was not enough, by itself, to serve as a safeguard against the potential dangers inherent in political power. The people

might become corrupted or demoralized or indifferent. Jefferson believed that the best practice for the avoidance of tyranny and the preservation of freedom was to follow two main policies. One was designed to limit power, and the other to control power.

14   In order to put limits on power, Jefferson felt, it was best to divide it by scattering its functions among as many entities as possible—among states, countries, and municipalities. In order to keep it in check, it was to be impartially balanced among legislative, executive, and judicial branches. Thus, no group, agency, or entity would be able legitimately to acquire sufficient power for abuse. This is, of course, the theory that is embedded in the Constitution and that underlies the American federal system with its "checks and balances".

15   For the control of power or, more specifically, the governmental apparatus itself, other devices had to be brought into play. Of these, two are of special importance: suffrage and elections.

16   Unlike many contemporaries, Jefferson believed in virtually universal suffrage. His opinion was that the universal right to vote was the only "rational and peaceable instrument" of free government.

17   Next to the right to vote, the system of free elections was the foremost instrument for control over government. This involved, first, the election by the people of practically all high government officials, and, secondly, fixed and regular periods of polling, established by law.

18   To make doubly sure that this mechanism would work as an effective control over power, Jefferson advocated frequent elections and short terms of office, so that the citizens would be enabled to express their "approbation or rejection" as soon as possible.

19   This, in substance, is the Jeffersonian philosophy—faith in the idea of equality, of freedom, and in the right of and need for popular control over government.

(1,134 words)

Words and Expressions

loom large			to assume great importance 显得重要
statesman	/ˈsteɪtsmən/	n.	a political or government leader, especially one who is respected as being wise, and fair 政治家
high-ranking	/ˌhaɪˈræŋkɪŋ/	adj.	having a high position in a government or other organization (在政府或其他机构中)级别(地位)高的
presidential	/ˌprezɪˈdenʃəl/	adj.	relating to a president 总统的,总统做的
philosopher	/fɪˈlɒsəfə/	n.	someone who thinks deeply about the world, life, etc. 思想家
democracy	/dɪˈmɒkrəsɪ/	n.	a system of government in which every citizen in the country can vote to elect its government officials 民主,民主政治,民主政体
postulate	/ˈpɒstjʊleɪt/	n.	something believed to be true, on which an argument or scientific discussion is based 假定,假设
reckon with			to consider 必须认真考虑(对待)
paramount	/ˈpærəmaʊnt/	adj.	more important than anything else 最重要的,至高无上的
premise	/ˈpremɪs/	n.	a statement or idea that you accept as true and use as a base for developing other ideas 前提
assign	/əˈsaɪn/	vt.	to fix or name 确定,指定
superstition	/ˌsuːpəˈstɪʃən/	n.	a belief that some objects or actions are lucky or unlucky, or that they cause events to happen, based on old ideas of magic 迷信
enlightenment	/ɪnˈlaɪtnmənt/	n.	the state of understanding something clearly, or the act of making someone understand something clearly 领悟,启发,开导
conception	/kənˈsepʃən/	n.	an idea about what something is like, or a general understanding of something 观念,思想
intertwined	/ˌɪntəˈtwaɪnd/	adj.	closely related 紧密相关的
unalienable	/ˌʌnˈeɪljənəbl/	adj.	unable to be removed 不可剥夺的
foremost	/ˈfɔːməʊst/	adj.	in a leading position among a group of people or things 最重要的

Unit 10 Famous People

untrammeled	/ˌʌnˈtræməld/	adj.	not limited by anyone or anything 不受限制的，不受妨碍的
undermine	/ˌʌndəˈmaɪn/	vt.	to gradually make someone or something less strong or effective 逐渐削弱，逐渐损害
paradox	/ˈpærədɒks/	n.	a situation that seems strange because it involves two ideas or qualities that are very different 矛盾 **paradoxical** adj. 矛盾的
ingrained	/ɪnˈɡreɪnd/	adj.	so firmly held that is not likely to change 根深蒂固的，难以改变的
hereditary	/hɪˈredɪtərɪ/	adj.	passed from one generation to following generations 世代沿袭的
monarchy	/ˈmɒnəkɪ/	n.	the system in which a country is ruled by a king or queen 君主制，君主政体
antipathy	/ænˈtɪpəθɪ/	n.	a feeling of strong dislike towards someone or something 厌恶，反感
be at variance with			to be different from（与某人/某物）有分歧（大相径庭）
vice versa		adv.	used to say that the opposite of a situation you have just described is also true 反之亦然
legitimate	/lɪˈdʒɪtɪmɪt/	adj.	① fair, correct, or reasonable according to accepted standards of behavior 合理的，正当的，公正的 ② correct, allowable, or operating according to the law 合法的，依法的 **legitimately** adv. 合法地，依法地
justification	/ˌdʒʌstɪfɪˈkeɪʃən/	n.	a good and acceptable reason for doing something 正当理由，可接受的理由
privileged	/ˈprɪvɪlɪdʒd/	adj.	having advantages because of your wealth, social position, etc.（因富有、有权势等而）有特权的
depository	/dɪˈpɒzɪtərɪ/	n.	a place where something can be safely kept 储藏室，仓库
monumental	/ˌmɒnjʊˈmentl/	adj.	very important, for an achievement, piece of work, etc. which is usually based on many years of work 丰碑式的，伟大而不朽的
capability	/ˌkeɪpəˈbɪlɪtɪ/	n.	the natural ability, skill, or power that makes a machine, person, or organization able to do something, especially something difficult 才

vigorously	/ˈvɪɡərəslɪ/	adv.	done with a lot of energy and strength or determination 强有力地
safeguard	/ˈseɪfɡɑːd/	n.	a rule, agreement, etc. that is intended to protect someone or something from possible dangers or problems 保障,保护措施
demoralize	/dɪˈmɒrəlaɪz/	vt.	to reduce or destroy someone's courage or confidence 使泄气(意志消沉) **demoralized** *adj.* 使泄气的
tyranny	/ˈtɪrənɪ/	n.	government by one person or a small group that has gained power unfairly and uses it in a cruel way 专制统治,暴政
preservation	/ˌprezəˈveɪʃən/	n.	the act of making sure that a situation continues without changing 维持,保护
scatter	/ˈskætə/	vt.	to throw something in different directions 散布,撒(某物)
municipality	/mjuːˌnɪsɪˈpælɪtɪ/	n.	a town, city, or other small area, which has its own government to make decisions about local affairs, or the officials in that government 市,自治市
keep something in check			to control something 控制某物
impartial	/ɪmˈpɑːʃəl/	adj.	not involved in a particular situation, and therefore able to give a fair opinion or piece of advice 公正的,不偏不倚的 **impartially** *adv.* 公正地,不偏不倚地
legislative branch			立法机关
executive branch			(批准决议和法律并负责实施的)政府的行政部门
judicial branch			司法部门
embed	/ɪmˈbed/	vt.	to make something an important or basic part of something else, or to make it difficult to remove 使深植于,使难以消除
apparatus	/ˌæpəˈreɪtəs/	n.	a system or process for doing something 机构,机制
device	/dɪˈvaɪs/	n.	a way of achieving a particular purpose 手段,方法
bring something into play			to use 利用某事物,使某事物发挥作用

Unit 10   Famous People

suffrage	/ˈsʌfrɪdʒ/	n.	the right to vote in national elections 选举权,投票权
contemporary	/kənˈtempərərɪ/	n.	someone who lived or was in a particular place at the same time as someone else 同时代的人,同辈
practically	/ˈpræktɪklɪ/	adv.	almost 几乎,差不多
polling	/ˈpəʊlɪŋ/	n.	when people vote in a political election (政治选举中的)投票
mechanism	/ˈmekənɪzəm/	n.	a system that is intended to achieve something or deal with a problem 机制,体制
approbation	/ˌæprəˈbeɪʃən/	n.	official praise or approval 称赞,认可,批准
rejection	/rɪˈdʒekʃən/	n.	the act of not accepting, believing in, or agreeing with something 拒绝

Reading Comprehension

I. What aspect of Thomas Jefferson's ideas is discussed in the text? And what message does the author convey to the readers?

_____
_____
_____
_____
_____

II. Answer the following questions.

1. What are the three paramount ideas in Thomas Jefferson's democracy?
2. How do you understand the sentence: "no definite limit could be assigned" to man's continued progress from ignorance and superstition to enlightenment and happiness (Para. 5)?
3. What did Thomas Jefferson mean by the concept of equality?
4. What did Jefferson mean by freedom and why was it necessary for him to claim it as an "inherent" or "natural" right?

5. According to Jefferson, how could government be prevented from swallowing the rights of the people?

6. What does "checks and balances" mean in the American federal system? What is your attitude towards this policy?

III. Judge, according to the text, whether the following statements are true or false. For false statements, write the facts in parentheses.

1. Thomas Jefferson is equally known as a statesman and a philosopher of democracy.
    (   )

2. Thomas Jefferson believed that equality was a political rather than a biological or psychological or economic conception.
    (   )

3. Even though some of Thomas Jefferson's beliefs in democracy were widely challenged and denied in his day, he still believed in the ideas.
    (   )

4. Confidence in the people serves as a unique power in safeguarding against the dangers existing in political power.
    (   )

5. Jefferson formulated the ideas of democracy with fullness, persuasiveness, and logic.
    (   )

6. According to Jefferson, the best practice to avoid tyranny and the preservation of freedom was to control the power of the government.
    (   )

7. Most people in Jefferson's day believed that everyone had the right to vote in political elections.
    (   )

IV. Paraphrase the following sentences within the context.

1. (Para. 2) Those interested in democracy as a political philosophy and system—even those who do not accept his postulates or are critical of his solutions—must reckon with his thought.

Unit 10　Famous People

2. (Para. 5) To Jefferson, it was virtually evident that the human being was essentially good, that he was capable of constant improvement through education and reason.

3. (Para. 7) In the *Declaration of Independence* he stated it as "self-evident" that liberty was one of the "inherent" and "unalienable rights" with which the Creator endowed man.

4. (Para. 8) Foremost in the area of individual liberty, Jefferson believed, was the untrammeled right to say, think, write, and believe whatever the citizen wishes—provided, of course, he does not directly injure his neighbors.

5. (Para. 9) Experience of the past, when governments were either too strong for the ruled or too weak to rule them, convinced Jefferson of the desirability of establishing a delicate natural balance between political power and personal rights.

6. (Para. 10) For the then-existing governments of Europe, virtually all of them hereditary monarchies, he had antipathy mixed with contempt.

7. (Para. 11) He began with the postulate that government existed for the people, and not vice versa; that it had no independent being except as an instrument of the people; and that it had no legitimate justifications for existence except to serve the people.

8. (Para. 12) This key idea in the Jeffersonian political universe rested on the monumental assumption that the people at large had the wisdom, the capability, and the knowledge exclusively to carry the burden of political power and responsibility.

9. (Para. 14) In order to keep it in check, it was to be impartially balanced among legislative, executive, and judicial branches.

Vocabulary Exercises

I. **Fill in each blank with one of the two words from each pair and note the difference of meaning between them. Change the form when necessary.**

1. ANTIPATHY   SYMPATHY

   a. The actor is a private man with a deep _____ towards the press.
   b. Of those people questioned, 53% said their _____ were with the Conservative Party.
   c. Despite the deep _____ between them, the two sides have managed to negotiate an agreement.
   d. What she needed at the moment was someone who would lend a(n) _____ ear to her.

2. POSTULATE   SUPPOSE

   a. It was the Greek astronomer, Ptolemy, who _____ that the Earth was at the centre of the universe.
   b. I _____ it's too late to apply for that job now.
   c. It has been _____ that changes in geography, climate, and sea levels were responsible for the extinction of dinosaurs.
   d. The meeting was _____ to take place on Tuesday.

3. PROCLAIM   EXCLAIM
   a. All the countries in this region have _____ their loyalty to the alliance.
   b. They _____ in delight upon hearing the good news.
   c. With a(n) _____ of disgust she turned the program off.
   d. She was _____ Queen at the age of 15 after the sudden death of her father.

II. **Fill in the blank in each sentence with a word or phrase taken from the box in its appropriate form.**

| desirability | intertwine | impartially | in substance | legitimate |
| ingrained | untrammeled | rest on | be at variance with | |

1. The prosperity of the city is inextricably _____ with the fortunes of these factories.
2. What she said, _____, was that the mayor should resign.
3. Christianity _____ the belief that Jesus was the son of God.
4. The government must ensure the independence and _____ of the justice system.
5. Self-governing schools are _____ by education authority rules.
6. Their house is in a very _____ area of the city.
7. Such prejudices are deeply _____ in the society and cannot be corrected easily.
8. Young people's reactions to the world are often _____ those of their parents.
9. The rebels regard the official parliament as _____.

III. **Choose a word or phrase that best completes each of the following sentences.**

1. According to a study, some researchers said that it was time to _____ the myth that geniuses were gifted or possessed inborn talent.
   A. acknowledge   B. demolish   C. conceive   D. proclaim
2. Every citizen in a democratic country may _____ the protection of the law.
   A. proclaim   B. announce   C. claim   D. renounce
3. The president's enemies are spreading rumors to _____ his authority.
   A. undermine   B. underlie   C. undertake   D. understand

4. Parents often faced the _____ between doing what they felt was good for the development of the child and what they could stand by way of undisciplined noise and destructiveness.

    A. paradox   B. junction   C. premise   D. dilemma

5. We're trying to bring out the _____ artistic talents that many people possess without realizing it.

    A. latent   B. salient   C. paramount   D. potential

6. We ought to put a strict limit _____ the amount of time we can spend on the project.

    A. to   B. of   C. on   D. in

Translation Exercises

Translate each of the following sentences into English, using the word or phrase given in the brackets.

1. 无论平民还是高官，法律面前一律平等，任何人都没有特权。(high-ranking)

2. 就豪华、可靠性和快捷程度而言，没有什么汽车能与宝马相媲美。(no other)

3. 丽莎一向对我们抚育孩子的方式吹毛求疵。但是，她当了母亲之后，态度就改变了。(be critical of)

4. 失业期间，他肩负的压力除了经济上的，还有来自父母的，两者不可避免地纠结在一起。(intertwine with)

5. 公司各部门的看法经常不一致，只让一个部门负责提出方案，其他部门会认为是对这个部门的偏袒。(in conflict)

6. 我不赞成在各个电视台做广告，因为大量的广告会激怒消费者，从而有损产品的形象。(undermine)

7. 一些地方官员向她提出的意见与总统的愿望相抵触，这使她陷入了困境。(at variance with)

Unit 10　Famous People

8. 你的假设有多处漏洞，因此你不能以它为依据来断定他就是当晚抢劫银行的夜贼。(rest on)

_____

Text II

Kings of Athletes

Pre-reading Questions

1. Who do you think are the most famous athletes? Why?
2. What kind of athlete can be addressed as a "king"? Why?

1   Under a scorching summer sun a dozen muscular men in their mid-20s sprint along a Santa Barbara, California, beach. On and on they run until exhaustion forces them to rest. Suddenly, a rough voice yells, "Remember the Olympics!" Dragging themselves to their feet, the 12 go back to their running. Finally, after a Spartan meal and a training film, they trot to a nearby field to practice jumping and pole vaulting as the sun goes down.

2   Following these athletes through their training day, you might think that they cannot decide which track event they want to compete in. They seem to practice just about everything! Yet there is purpose here. Each of these men—like hundreds of others around the world—is determined to prove that he is an unbeatable one-man track and field team. He hopes to compete as one of his country's three representatives in the decathlon event during the Olympic Games.

3   The Olympic decathlon is recognized as the most demanding test of individual athletic ability there is. It decides who is the world's greatest all-around athlete. The present-day decathlon began in a contest held at the 708 B.C. Olympiad to single out Greece's most perfect physical specimen. The decathlon (the word comes from Greek *deka*, "ten," and *athlon*, "contest") calls for an athlete to take part

in ten events in just two days. He must sprint 100 meters, long-jump, throw a 16-pound shot, high-jump, race 400 meters, scamper the 110-meter high hurdles, sling the discus, pole-vault, throw the javelin and top off everything by running 1,500 meters (nearly a mile). The order is arranged to keep him from using essentially the same motion twice in a row.

4   Just enduring this punishing routine is enough to leave a decathloner quivering with fatigue and 12 to 15 pounds lighter through dehydration. But it's not enough to guarantee him a respectable finish. Why? He must come up with top marks under a complicated, 78-page scoring system that is based not only on how well he does against his opponents in each event but also on how his effort compares with the latest standard for that event.

5   Because of these herculean demands, few sports authorities, if any, would say that the greatest professional baseball, football, basketball or hockey stars could match decathlon champions for stamina or strength. In Germany a decathlon champion is correctly hailed as *König der Athleten*—king of athletes.

6   Years of training are the lot of an aspiring decathlon champ. He must carefully balance his overall conditioning to build one of sport's rarest physiques. Extra-powerful shoulders that could give him an edge in throwing the discus and shot can slow him down in the sprints and hurdles. Thus, he must try to keep the tight, tapered calves of a sprinter even as he builds up a barrel chest to pump air for endurance races and a boxer's muscles for throwing the discus, shot and javelin.

7   After daily workouts, he usually keeps to a tissue-building diet. Some decathloner's eating choices might make other men sick to their stomachs. One places great faith in his secret formula of vegetables, raw looking beef and toasted sunflower seeds. Another breakfast on seven different vitamins followed by raw eggs, powdered milk, soybean oil, dehydrated liver and two calcium compounds—all mixed together.

8   However carefully conditioned an athlete may be, he also needs great self-discipline during competition. Few decathloners ever showed this more dramatically than Bob Mathias during the 1948 Olympics in London. (He was a strapping 17-year-old California high-school student at the time.) A cold, driving rain had chased away all but a few hundred of the 70,000 spectators in dark, foggy Wembley Stadium by the time the pole vault was announced. The men in charge tied a white handkerchief to the crossbar to make it possible for

the contestants to see it.

9 Trying to keep the narrow lead he had gained by winning the seventh event, the discus throw, the little-known Mathias took a big chance. To save his strength, he tried none of the customary practice vaults. And he passed up his regular turns until the bar was set at ten feet.

10 If he failed at this height, he would lose so many points that he could never win the ten-event contest. Not the least bit bothered, Mathias charged down the runway, drilled his slippery pole into the muddy vaulting box and sprang skyward. Flawlessly he twisted over the bar. His later vaults won him a tie for second place in this event.

11 The veteran decathlon men knew that they had been outsmarted by a youngster. As a flashlight lit the dark foul line, Mathias then threw the javelin so far that he became just about unbeatable. Mud-splattered, suffering from both stomach and foot cramps, he was still able to score enough points in the 1,500 meter run to become the youngest man ever to win the Olympic decathlon.

12 Four years later, at Helsinki, Mathias triumphed again. He became the only man to win the Olympic decathlon twice. Asked if he wasn't really worried despite the calm that he showed during both Olympics, Mathias said, "You don't get any points for worrying."

13 Indeed, a decathlon star learns to put up with the pain and illness that often torment an over-trained body. Consider 190-pound William Toomey, a junior-high-school English teacher in Santa Barbara. Vowing in 1964 to win the 1968 Olympics in Mexico City, Toomey trained relentlessly. Meanwhile, he suffered bouts with mononucleosis and hepatitis, calcium deposits in his heels, a wrenched back. Add to the list a torn hamstring muscle, an ugly cut in his right calf that called for 35 stitches and surgery to remove bone fragments from his right knee.

14 In Mexico City, Toomey tore a hip muscle before the decathlon got under way. Knowing that Olympic rules forbid pain-killing drugs before competing, he set his alarm for dawn each day, in order to exercise the sore hip bit by bit until he could run. Between events, he held an ice pack on the bad hip. Then, before cheering crowds, he ran harder, leaped and vaulted higher, and threw farther than any of his opponents. Toomey won the gold medal—the oldest person (at 29) ever to do so. In the process, he set a new Olympic record for total points. "Behind every good decathlon man," he said later, "there is a world of injuries—

and a good doctor!"

15   These one-man teams fully live up to the Olympic spirit of sport for its own sake. Upon winning the 1960 Olympic decathlon, Rafer Johnson turned down offers from professional football and basketball teams. A trim 15 pounds lighter now than during his Olympic days, he still practices decathlon events. People often ask him why he never went after a profitable career as a pro athlete. He answers, "My goal in sports was never money. When you've won the Olympic decathlon, there is no other sport. It's time for something else." (Now a telephone-company executive, he gives much time to mentally retarded youngsters.)

16   Likewise, after his twin Olympic victories, Mathias turned down an offer from pro football's Washington Red-skins. Instead, he spent 2 and a half years in the Marines. Then he toured 35 countries for the State Department. When in 1966 he ran for a seat in Congress, politicians reminded him that he would have to defeat a man who had been 14 years in office. "One thing the decathlon teaches you," Mathias replied, "is that you can't win anything with shortcuts." Visiting almost every farm, vineyard and orchard in his district of California, Mathias went on to win the election handily.

17   Bill Toomey, who has helped many an upcoming decathloner and set the point-total record at which they are all aiming, sums up the credo of these super-athletes, "In the decathlon, you don't need cheers, headlines or even anyone to watch you perform. It's like religion, painting or poetry. There's enough satisfaction just doing it."

(1,323 words)

Reading Comprehension

I. **Answer the following questions with the information you read from the passage.**

   1. According to the text, what is the toughest track and field event in the Olympic Games? Why?
   2. What does the word "decathlon" mean? What events are included in decathlon?
   3. Why does the author say some decathletes' diets make other men sick to their stomachs?

4. What did Mathias do to save his strength for the vaults during the 1948 Olympics in London? Did it work?

5. What can people learn from the decathletes, such as Bill Toomey, Rafer Johnson, Mathias, etc.?

6. What is the credo of these super-athletes?

II. **Topics for discussion and reflection.**

1. A decathlon athlete competes against himself and the scoring table with what coaches refer to as "decathlon mentality". What qualities does decathlon mentality include?

2. Do you think a decathlete will be successful if he applies "decathlon mentality" to his later career? Why or why not?

Exercises for Integrated Skills

I. **Dictation**

Listen to the following passage. Altogether the passage will be read to you four times. During the first reading, which will be read at normal speed, listen and try to understand the meaning. For the second and third readings, the passage will be read sentence by sentence, or phrase by phrase, with intervals of 15 to 20 seconds. The last reading will be done at normal speed again and during this time you should check your work. You will then be given 2 minutes to check through your work once more.

II. Cloze

Fill in each blank in the passage below with a word or phrase taken from the box in its appropriate form.

infect	endorse	chant	season	tolerate
foul	count	all-out	goalie	youngster
agile	gasoline	tradition	score	nickname
popular	millionaire	precious	overwhelm	revolutionize

The Black Pearl

Pele wore uniform number 10 and played left inside forward. With his ___1___, speed and incredible ball-handling skills, he ___2___ soccer, instigating a creative, ___3___ attack that became the Brazilian style and was much more exciting for casual fans than the ___4___ defense-oriented game. During Pele's career, he scored five goals or more in a game on six occasions, scored four goals in 30 games, and had 92 games with three goals. Three times he scored more than 100 goals in a ___5___.

Pele acquired several ___6___ during his career: "___7___" for his energy, "The Executioner" for his brilliant ability to finish an offensive drive and put the ball in the net, and, most ___8___, "The Black Pearl," because he was ___9___. On the field, his joy at playing the game he loved was obvious and ___10___. Pele would salute the crowd after ___11___ a goal and, on many occasions, the goalkeeper he had just beaten would wave or bow to him. If a keeper stopped his shot, Pele would often shake hands with him. When he scored, thousands of fans would stand and ___12___ his name.

Pele had ___13___ tricks to get around defenders. He developed incredible shots, including a swerving shot from 40 yards out that would curve away from the ___14___ at the last second, and a drop shot that would appear to be going over the crossbar and then dip into the net. Often, defenders would be all over Pele, and he would be ___15___ and harassed. After years of ___16___ this treatment, he began to retaliate and draw yellow cards himself. After an Argentinean player repeatedly kicked him and spat at him, Pele kicked back.

The first soccer player to become a ___17___, Pele ___18___ with offers

Unit 10 Famous People

to make personal appearances and sign business deals, but he refused to _____ __19__ cigarettes or liquor. "I know that I have influence on __20__ and I don't feel that I want them to think if I should endorse these products I want them to use them," he said, according to Marcus's book.

Oral Activities

Activity One: Work in groups and discuss the following questions.

1. What qualities do your heroes or idols have in common? Are they all famous people? What do you think makes people famous?
2. Name some of the most influential people in history or nowadays. How do they exert influences in certain fields?
3. Do you wish to be a famous person? What problems do famous people have to face?

Activity Two: Star Power

   Superstars influence millions of people every day. They influence popular fashions and the way people dress. They even influence the products people decide to buy. But increasingly, celebrities are also using their fame to make a positive difference in the world. Publicity follows famous people, no matter where they go or what they do. When famous people give their opinions, many people follow.

   For celebrities, the public is either too superstitious or too critical. Do you think stars should act as perfect role models? Should we pay special attention to their remarks or actions? Work in groups and present your viewpoints in different forms. It can be Q and A, short play, interview, etc.

Writing Practice

Note Writing: Describing People
   During the Olympics, you were very lucky to see your dream idol, a sports star. Write an informal letter to tell your friend about your excitement, describe you dream idol, and focus on your impression of him/her.

23 August, 2008

Dear _____,

Yours,

Composition Writing

As discussed in the oral activities, stars/celebrities influence millions of people every day. Almost everyone has his/her own idol. But, there are many famous actors, singers, sports figures who fail the public, or their fans. Do you think they have a responsibility as role models? What do you think are the reasons why they fail to be role models? Write a composition to express your idea in about 120 words.

Unit 11 Health

Warm-up Activities

1. Happy Health Hour
   Organize a Health Hour activity in your class. Work in groups to finish the tasks.

   Task 1: Prepare a lecture on health. Here are some roles you can play and some lecture themes you can choose from.

Roles	Lecture Themes
A medical doctor	Prevention of colds / food poisoning / sports injuries
A psychologist	Stress and ways of reducing and preventing it
A fitness coach	Fast and healthy weight loss

   Task 2: Make a list of questions that the audience might ask the lecturer after the presentation.

Text I

Models of Health

Pre-reading Questions

1. How do you define health? Does it mean not being sick, feeling good, or something else?
2. What do you think about the current state of China's health-care system? How can it be improved?

1   Scientists and health educators have developed three main ways to define health: the medical model, the environmental model, and the wellness, or holistic model. How you approach being healthy and well in many ways depends on your personal definition of health.

2   The medical model's main tenet is that health is the absence of one or more of the "five Ds"—death, disease, discomfort, disability, and dissatisfaction. In other words, if you are not sick or dying, you are considered to be in the best attainable state of health. Followers of the medical model rely almost exclusively on biological explanations of disease and illness and tend to interpret disease and illness in terms of malfunction of individual organs, cells, and other biological systems, e.g., liver disease, heart disease, or sickle cell anemia.

3   Within the medical model, the health of a population is measured in terms of vital statistics, which are data on the degree of illness (morbidity) and the numbers of deaths (mortality) in a given population. Vital statistics include prevalence (the predominance of a disease in a population) and incidence (the frequency at which certain diseases occur). These statistical measurements allow comparisons between populations and also within the same population over time.

4   The medical model tends not to deal with social problems that affect health and only with difficulty, integrates mental and behavioral issues that do not derive from diseased organs. In the medical model, health is restored by curing a disease or by restoring function to a damaged body part. Because of its exclusive focus on biological processes, the medical model is of limited value. It does not help us understand psychological and social factors that affect health and contribute to disease.

5   The reliance on biological interpretations of illness has contributed greatly to the success of the medical model. Anyone who has been cured of a serious infection by taking antibiotics or undergone a lifesaving surgical procedure can attest to that. On the other hand, that same reliance on biological thinking has not furthered understanding of health and illness in terms of psychological and social factors, nor has it been very successful in fostering health by preventing

disease caused by unhealthy lifestyles and destructive behaviors.

6   The environmental model of health emerged with modern analyses of ecosystems and environmental risks to human health. In this model, health is defined in terms of the quality of a person's adaptation to the environment as conditions change. This model includes the effects on personal health of socioeconomic status, education, and multiple environmental factors.

7   Unlike the medical model, which focuses on diseased organs and biological abnormalities, the environmental model focuses on conditions outside the individual that affect his or her health. These conditions include the quality of air and water, living conditions, exposure to harmful substances, socioeconomic conditions, social relationships, and the health-care system.

8   In many respects the environmental model of health is similar to ancient Asian and Native American philosophies that associate health with harmonious interactions with fellow creatures and the environment. In particular, as the environment changes, one's interaction with it must change to remain in harmony. Illness is interpreted as disharmony of human and environmental interactions.

9   The holistic or wellness model defines health in terms of the whole person, not in terms of diseased parts of the body. The holistic model encompasses the physiological, mental, emotional, social, spiritual, and environmental aspects of individuals and communities. It focuses on optimal health, prevention of disease, and positive mental and emotional states.

10   The holistic model incorporates the idea of spiritual health, which is not considered in the medical model. Unlike the medical model, which assumes that a person who is not sick or not suffering from a disease is as healthy as possible, the holistic model proposes that health is a state of optimum or positive wellness.

11   Wellness is much more than physical health; it addresses mental, emotional, and spiritual aspects of a person, as well as the relationships among these dimensions. The wellness continuum helps delineate between the medical concept of health and the wellness concept. Most people find themselves in the neutral area of the continuum. Most of us, however, can remember moving toward disability and also moving toward optimal health or high-level wellness.

12   One may move from a state of illness or disease back to the neutral point many times with the help of medical care. The wellness continuum also includes

prevention, which means taking positive actions to prevent acute and chronic illnesses.

13   Wellness is not static; it is a dynamic process that takes into account all the decisions we make daily, such as which foods we eat, the amount of exercise we get, whether we drink alcohol before driving, wear safety belts, or smoke cigarettes. Every choice we make potentially affects health and wellness.

14   The models themselves are abstractions of ideas, but in real life one needs to use whatever is practical to optimize health and well-being. Health depends very much on each person's perception. People with a disease may live joyful, positive, healthy lives; people without a disease may be despondent, unhappy, and feel sick. People need attainable goals to promote wellness and to live harmoniously with family, friends, and the environment.

15   Truth does not change over time. Jesse Williams, one of the founders of modern health education, described health as "that condition of the individual that makes possible the highest enjoyment of life, the greatest constructive work, and that shows itself in the best service to the world.... Health as freedom from disease is a standard of mediocrity; health as a quality of life is a standard of inspiration and increasing achievement."

16   This is a goal we believe in, and the view we reflect.

(946 words)

Words and Expressions

wellness	/ˈwelnɪs/	n.	the state of being healthy 健康
holistic	/həʊˈlɪstɪk/	adj.	considering a person or thing as a whole, rather than as separate parts 整体的，全面的
tenet	/ˈtenɪt/	n.	a principle or belief, especially one that is part of a larger system of beliefs 信条，信念，教义
discomfort	/dɪsˈkʌmfət/	n.	a feeling of slight pain or of being physically uncomfortable 不适
attainable	/əˈteɪnəbəl/	adj.	capable of being attained or accomplished 可以达到的，可以获得的
exclusive	/ɪkˈskluːsɪv/	adj.	excluding all but the thing specified 唯一的 **exclusively** adv. 仅仅，不过

Unit 11 Health

biological	/ˌbaɪəˈlɒdʒɪkəl/	adj.	relating to biology or the natural processes performed by living things 生物学的，生物的
malfunction	/mælˈfʌŋkʃən/	n.	a fault in the way a machine or part of someone's body works 功能障碍，疾病，故障
liver	/ˈlɪvə/	n.	a large organ in your body that produces bile and cleans your blood（人体的）肝脏
sickle cell anemia			镰刀形红细胞贫血症
morbidity	/mɔːˈbɪdɪtɪ/	n.	the relative incidence of a particular disease 发病率
mortality	/mɔːˈtælɪtɪ/	n.	the number of deaths during a particular period of time among a particular type or group of people 死亡率
prevalence	/ˈprevələns/	n.	the total number of cases of a disease or event in a given population at a specific time 疾病的流行程度
predominance	/prɪˈdɒmɪnəns/	n.	the state of being predominant over others 支配地位，主导地位
incidence	/ˈɪnsɪdəns/	n.	the number of times something happens, especially something bad（尤指坏事的）发生率
frequency	/ˈfriːkwənsɪ/	n.	the number of times that something happens within a particular period of time or within a particular group of people 发生率，频率，发生的次数
statistical	/stəˈtɪstɪkl/	adj.	of or relating to statistics 统计的，统计学的
measurement	/ˈmeʒəmənt/	n.	the act of measuring something 测量，计量
integrate	/ˈɪntɪɡreɪt/	vt.	to combine two or more things in order to become more effective 使结合，使合并
infection	/ɪnˈfekʃən/	n.	a disease that affects a particular part of the body and is caused by bacteria or a virus 感染
antibiotic	/ˌæntɪbaɪˈɒtɪk/	n.	a drug that is used to kill bacteria and cure infections 抗生素，抗菌素
undergo	/ˌʌndəˈɡəʊ/	vt.	to experience something which is unpleasant or which involves a change 经受，经历，遭受
surgical	/ˈsɜːdʒɪkəl/	adj.	relating to or used for medical operations 外科手术的，外科的

attest	/əˈtest/	vi./vt.	to show or prove that something is true 证明，作为(……的)证据
further	/ˈfɜːðə/	vt.	to help something succeed or be achieved 促进，推动
destructive	/dɪˈstrʌktɪv/	adj.	causing damage to people or things 毁坏性的，造成破坏的
ecosystem	/ˈiːkəʊˌsɪstəm/	n.	all the animals and plants in a particular area, and the way in which they are related to each other and to their environment 生态系统
socioeconomic	/ˌsəʊsiəʊˌiːkəˈnɒmɪk/	adj.	based on a combination of social and economic conditions 社会经济的
abnormality	/ˌæbnɔːˈmælɪti/	n.	an abnormal feature, especially something that is wrong with part of someone's body 反常，变态，畸形
exposure	/ɪkˈspəʊzə/	n.	the state of being put into a harmful or bad situation or position without having any protection against what may happen 暴露，显露
substance	/ˈsʌbstəns/	n.	a particular type of solid, liquid, or gas 物质
philosophy	/fɪˈlɒsəfi/	n.	the attitude or set of ideas that guides the behaviour of a person or organization 观点，宗旨，见解
encompass	/ɪnˈkʌmpəs/	vt.	to include a wide range of ideas, subjects, etc. 包括，包含
physiological	/ˌfɪziəˈlɒdʒɪkəl/	adj.	of or consistent with an organism's normal functioning 生理的，生理机能的
optimal	/ˈɒptɪməl/	adj.	the best or most suitable 最佳的，最适宜的
incorporate	/ɪnˈkɔːpəreɪt/	vt.	to include something as part of a group, system, plan, etc. 包含，并入
propose	/prəˈpəʊz/	vt.	to suggest an idea, method etc as an answer to a scientific question or as a better way of doing something 提出(某观点、方法等)
optimum	/ˈɒptɪməm/	adj.	the best or most suitable option for a particular purpose or in a particular situation 最佳的，最适宜的
address	/əˈdres/	vt.	to give attention to or deal with a matter or problem 把注意力放在，处理

wellness continuum			健康连续相
delineate	/dɪˈlɪnɪeɪt/	vt.	to describe or draw something carefully so that people can understand it 描写, 描绘, 刻画
neutral	/ˈnjuːtrəl/	adj.	lacking distinguishing quality or characteristics 不确定的, 模糊的
chronic	/ˈkrɒnɪk/	adj.	(especially of a disease or something bad) continuing for a long time 慢性的, 长期的
static	/ˈstætɪk/	adj.	not moving, changing, or developing 不变化的, 不动的
take something into account			把某事考虑在内
potentially	/pəˈtenʃəlɪ/	adv.	possibly 可能地, 潜在地
abstraction	/æbˈstrækʃən/	n.	a general idea about a type of situation, thing, or person rather than a specific example from real life 抽象概念
optimize	/ˈɒptɪmaɪz/	vt.	to improve the way that something is done or used so that it is as effective as possible 使最优化, 使最有效
despondent	/dɪˈspɒndənt/	adj.	extremely unhappy and without hope 沮丧的, 失望的
mediocrity	/ˌmiːdɪˈɒkrɪtɪ/	n.	ordinariness as a consequence of being average and not outstanding 平常, 平凡, 平庸

Notes:

A health care system is an arrangement in which health care is delivered. There are many variations of health care systems around the world.

Reading Comprehension

I. **Summarize the main idea for each part into one or two sentences.**
    Part. 1 (Para. 1)

    _____
    _____
    _____

Part. 2 (Para. 2–Para. 5)

_____
_____

Part. 3 (Para. 6–Para. 8)

_____
_____

Part. 4 (Para. 9–Para. 13)

_____
_____

Part. 5 (Para. 14–end)

_____
_____

II. Answer the following questions.

1. According to scientists and health educators, what are the three models to define health?
2. What do the "five Ds" stand for? Explain them according to your understanding of the medical model of health.
3. In which aspect is the medical model different from the environmental model in defining health?
4. What does wellness include?
5. How does the article define wellness as a dynamic process?

III. Judge, according to the text, whether the following statements are true or false. For false statements, write the facts in parentheses.

1. The core of the medical model is that health is the presence of one or more of the "five Ds".
   (   )
2. Like the medical model, the environmental model focuses on conditions outside the individual.
   (   )

3. Because of its significant focus on biological processes, the medical model is of great value.
   (　　　　　　　　　　　　　　　　　　　　　　　　　　　　　　　　)

4. In the medical model, health is defined in terms of the quality of a person's adaptation to the outside world as surroundings change.
   (　　　　　　　　　　　　　　　　　　　　　　　　　　　　　　　　)

5. Illness is interpreted as disharmony of human and environmental interactions according to some health educators.
   (　　　　　　　　　　　　　　　　　　　　　　　　　　　　　　　　)

6. Wellness means the physical, emotional, and spiritual well-being rather than the physical state of a person.
   (　　　　　　　　　　　　　　　　　　　　　　　　　　　　　　　　)

7. What we eat and drink influences our health and wellness.
   (　　　　　　　　　　　　　　　　　　　　　　　　　　　　　　　　)

IV. Paraphrase the following sentences within the context.

1. (Para. 2) The medical model's main tenet is that health is the absence of one or more of the "five Ds" — death, disease, discomfort, disability, and dissatisfaction.

2. (Para. 4) The medical model tends not to deal with social problems that affect health and only with difficulty integrates mental and behavioral issues that do not derive from diseased organs.

3. (Para. 5) The reliance on biological interpretations of illness has contributed greatly to the success of the medical model. Anyone who has been cured of a serious infection by taking antibiotics or undergone a lifesaving surgical procedure can attest to that.

4. (Para. 10) Unlike the medical model, which assumes that a person who is not sick or not suffering from a disease is as healthy as possible, the holistic model proposes that health is a state of optimum or positive wellness.

5. (Para. 11) Wellness is much more than physical health; it addresses mental, emotional, and spiritual aspects of a person, as well as the relationships among these dimensions.

6. (Para. 15) Health as freedom from disease is a standard of mediocrity; health as a quality of life is a standard of inspiration and increasing achievement.

Vocabulary Exercises

I. Fill in the blank in each sentence with a word or phrase taken from the box. Change the form where necessary.

> optimize   despondent   attainable   holistic   delineate
> mediocrity   abnormality   morbidity   foster   prevalence

1. Parents should give correct guidance to children and _____ a sense of competition and cooperation.
2. More and more women are _____ positions of power in modern society.
3. The _____ of available resources is extremely important for ensuring sustainable development.
4. Ecological problems usually require _____ solutions.
5. His head was full of _____ fascination with other people's suffering.
6. She thought the film's plot was predictable and the acting was _____.
7. Those diseases are more _____ among young children.

8. An increasing number of tests are available for detecting genetic _____ in the fetus.
9. The boundary of the parking lot is _____ by a low brick wall.
10. He grew increasingly _____ when she failed to return his e-mails.

II. **Choose a word or phrase that best completes each of the following sentences.**

1. As a defense against air-pollution damage, many plants and animals release a(n) _____ to absorb harmful chemicals.
   A. essence   B. substance   C. stuff   D. material
2. The new government promises to _____ the economy to full strength.
   A. restore   B. regain   C. rebuild   D. repair
3. Daily insulin _____ is necessary for some diabetics.
   A. affection   B. fraction   C. infection   D. injection
4. While trying to _____ her phone, she caused a serious car accident.
   A. retrieve   B. punch   C. encompass   D. impulse
5. Standing alone, she gazed at the immense _____ of blue sky.
   A. dimension   B. expanse   C. extent   D. measure
6. One big mistake is you have placed too much reliance _____ her ideas and expertise.
   A. in   B. at   C. by   D. on
7. The number of terrorist attacks has increased _____ a terrifying degree.
   A. with   B. by   C. in   D. to
8. Even a brief exposure _____ radiation is very dangerous to your health.
   A. of   B. in   C. to   D. under

Translation Exercises

Translate each of the following sentences into English, using the word or phrase given in the brackets.

1. 在收入方面，这份工作并不能给我过高的回报，但我从中获得了宝贵的工作经验。(in terms of)

2. 两国首脑这次会谈的目的是消除昔日的误会,恢复两国之间的贸易关系。(restore)

3. 政府发布的《吸烟与健康报告》指出,抽烟是导致肺癌的主要原因。(contribute to)

4. 我希望你能与我的推荐人联系,他们会对我的学习成绩、职业道德和敬业精神提供证明。(attest to)

5. 就像欧洲的拉丁语和希腊语一样,梵语(Sanskrit)在印度和东南亚的地位非常重要,是印度传统文化的核心部分。(be similar to)

6. 他们担心工人们会将这一新的法律理解为限制他们的权利。(interpret as)

7. 我们不仅要考虑商品的内在质量与外观形态,也要考虑顾客的品位要求。(take into account)

8. 联合国成立60多年来,在推动世界和平与发展的事业中发挥了不可替代的作用。(further)

Text II

In Sickness, in Health

Pre-reading Questions

1. How can people live a healthier and happier life? Share your ideas with a partner.
2. Who plays a key role in saving the people who suffer fatal diseases, the doctor or the family?

Unit 11 Health

1   The year 1998 was the beginning of a remarkable transformation for my family. My father, Jim Dineen, the always healthy, weightlifting, never-missed-a-day-of-work kind of dad, discovered he had kidney disease. He was 52, and had no symptoms. We don't really know how he got it—he even guessed that exposure to Agent  Orange when he was in Vietnam could have been a factor—and the road to recovery has been long. But in November 2003, my father received a healthy kidney at Christ Hospital in Cincinnati, where my parents live. My mom, Joyce, a year his junior, was his donor. After years of marital ups and downs, multiple surgeries for complications of the disease, and financial challenges by the dozens, our family dynamic changed for all of us in ways we never could have expected.

2   My parents have certainly had their troubles, and as their child I'll never know how they made it to 38 years of marriage. They loved each other, but they didn't seem to like each other very much. Dad was too fond of his beer, and he talked down to Mom a lot. When she tried to stand up to him, a fight would inevitably follow. I remember Mom once coming to visit my sister Leslie and me when we were both attending Miami University of Ohio. She told us she and Dad were splitting. But ultimately, our parents stayed together because of their faith. They believed somehow that God had a reason for them to remain married, and resigned themselves to sharing their lives, however imperfectly it was.

3   It was my dad's disease that began to change things. In the beginning of his illness, he went through hell. In 1999, his electrolytes plummeted so low as a result of diuretics he was taking that he passed out and fell in the bathtub, fracturing both elbows and several ribs and suffering a concussion. He had been put on the steroid prednisone, and initially gained 40 pounds of fluid and almost lived in the bathroom.

4   Dad was self-conscious about his appearance, waiting until night to go out for groceries, and even then using the drive-through lane. The only time he really appeared in public in two years was at a wedding. Dad wanted to be there so much that he was willing to risk ridicule. (The only clothes he had at home

that would fit his swollen body were a gray sweat suit and slippers.) I don't know where he found the strength to go on.

5   During it all, my mother stood by, sympathetic and helpful. She was at his side through six stomach surgeries and 35 more procedures to drain fluid that had collected in his abdomen from the prednisone. He and Mom had to work as a team just to get him through the day.

6   The dialysis treatments, which began in 2001, first took place in a clinic three days a week. Dad's arm turned black from the needles. It's no wonder Mom felt terrified when he was approved for at-home dialysis—putting the procedure, and his health, in their hands. Still, she was adamant about not letting him go through it alone. Each night, just like a first officer with the captain of an airliner, Mom went over his checklist with him step by step. At one point when his muscles atrophied, perhaps as a result of the prednisone, she taught him how to walk again. The process seemed to go on and on, tying them both to the house and robbing them of so much freedom.

7   The decision to go ahead with a transplant for my father was a long and arduous one, mostly because he had liver damage too. One physician's assistant told him, "According to your file, you're supposed to be dead." And for a while, doctors mistakenly thought that he would need not just a kidney transplant, but a liver transplant too. Dad's future hung in limbo.

8   When the donor testing process finally began in the spring of 2003, numerous people including myself, my uncle Tom, and my Mom, came back as matches of varying degrees. But Mom was the one who insisted on going further. She said she wasn't scared, and it was the right thing to do. We all stepped back in amazement.

9   At last a date was chosen—November 11, 2003. All of a sudden, the only thing that seemed to matter to Dad was telling the world what a wonderful thing Mom was doing for him. A month before the surgery, he sent her birthday flowers with a note that read, "I love you and I love your kidney! Thank you!"

10 Financially, the disease was devastating to them. Because he was too sick to work, Dad lost his consulting business; throughout the same period, Mom was downsized from two different jobs. So for months they had no income and were in real danger of losing their house. My father had given up his leased car, and when Mom's stopped running, they had to somehow buy two cars, which was another big drain on their already taxed resources. So my sister and I were

humbled and surprised when, shortly before his surgery day, Dad handed us a diamond pendant that we were to give to Mom after the operation. He'd squirreled away his spare dollars to buy it.

11   At the hospital on the day of the transplant, all our relatives and friends gathered in the waiting room and became embroiled in a mean euchre tournament. My family has always handled things with a lot of laughter, and even though we were all tense, everybody was taking bets on how long this "change of demeanor" would last in my parents.

12   We'd informed Dad that if he chose to act like a real pain on any particular day after the operation, he wasn't allowed to blame it on PMS just because he'd now have a female kidney!

13   The surgeries went well, and not long afterward, my sister and I were allowed to go in to visit. Dad was in a great deal of pain but, again, all he could talk about was Mom. Was she okay? How was she feeling? Then the nurses let us do something unorthodox. As they were wheeling Mom out of the recovery room, they rolled her into a separate alcove to visit Dad. It was surreal to see both our parents hooked up to IVs and machines and trying to talk to each other through tears. The nurses allowed us to present the diamond pendant to Mom so that Dad could watch her open it. Everybody was crying, even the nurses.

14   As I stood with my digital camera in hand, I tried to keep the presence of mind to document the moment. My dad was having a hard time fighting back emotion, and suddenly my parents spontaneously reached out to hold each other's hands.

15   In my nearly 35 years of existence, I'd never seen my parents do that, and I was spellbound. I snapped a picture and later rushed home to make sure I'd captured that enormous, life-defining moment. That photo of my parents' hands said everything. After so many years of discord, it was apparent to me that they finally understood how much each loved the other.

16   My father stopped drinking early in his disease, and he has started back to the health club again to improve his muscle tone. He's fascinated by how quickly he has recovered physically. But I have seen so many more profound changes. It's as if the transplant healed our whole family.

17   There's definitely been a softening of Dad. He's mellowed, and he has more patience now. He's not condescending to my mother anymore. Mom, too, has loosened up, since she's not dealing with all that anger. There's a closeness

that they didn't have before, and the experience has deepened their faith. Mom says she can see God's hand in this all along the way.

18   I live in Nashville, and when I talk with my parents on the phone now, I joke and say, "Who are you people? You're freaking me out!" because at times they act like kids. They laugh more and complain less.

19   For Christmas, Leslie and I gave them two framed photos linked together by hooks. The top photo is of their clasped hands on their wedding day, August 7, 1965. Handwritten on the matting it says, "For better or worse, for richer or poorer." The second photo is of that day in the recovery room. Their hands are intertwined with hospital bands and IVs, and on the matting it says, "In sickness and in health, 'til death do us part."

(1,443 words)

Reading Comprehension

I. Answer the following questions with the information you read from the passage.

1. When Dad got the kidney disease, was it easy for him to recover from it?
2. Before Dad got the disease, how was his relationship with Mom in their daily life?
3. Why did the physician's assistant say Dad was supposed to be dead?
4. What played an essential role in Dad's rehabilitation?
5. Explain the proverb, "Misfortune tests the sincerity of friends." with the story you just read.

II. Topics for discussion and reflection.

1. More and more attention is being paid to mental health in China. How can people strengthen their mental health?
2. Mark Twain said, "The only way to keep your health is to eat what you don't want, drink what you don't like, and do what you'd rather not." Do you think you can achieve sound health by following Mark Twain's advice?

Unit 11 Health

Exercises for Integrated Skills

I. Dictation

Listen to the following passage. Altogether the passage will be read to you four times. During the first reading, which will be read at normal speed, listen and try to understand the meaning. For the second and third readings, the passage will be read sentence by sentence, or phrase by phrase, with intervals of 15 to 20 seconds. The last reading will be done at normal speed again and during this time you should check your work. You will then be given 2 minutes to check through your work once more.

_____

_____

_____

_____

_____

II. Cloze

Fill in each blank in the passage below with a word or phrase taken from the box in its appropriate form.

short-lived	immune	slow	stress	equivalent
investigate	decrease	overall	trace	equivocal
document	stimulus	yield	adage	commission
contract	surprising	confirm	relation	complement

We have all heard the old ___1___ before: laughter is the best medicine. But, it might just be among the oldest medicine. In a report published by the University of Wolverhampton, and ___2___ by the British television channel Dave, the world's oldest joke can be ___3___ back to 1900 BC. Not ___4___, the list of the world's top 10 oldest jokes includes the ever-popular bathroom humor and much sexual innuendo. Empirical medical research ___5___ that people who smile and laugh are generally happy, and people who do not, are not. The benefits of humor and laughter as ___6___ medicine, as well as just a healthy life practice, are ___7___. As far back as the second century AD, Greek physicians ___8___ that people who developed certain diseases had "melancholic" personalities. More recent clinicians have produced anecdotal reports of people developing cancer during ___9___ life events. Humor can be used to decrease stress, reduce pain, and increase ___10___ function, but just how laughter elicits a physiologic response is still under ___11___.

Laughter is a naturally occurring response to humorous ___12___ and is a rather easily implemented and cost-effective clinical tool. Some publications even report that laughter is ___13___ to aerobic exercise. It is true that laughter can increase blood flow, stimulate circulation, ___14___ muscle groups, and improve respiratory function. But, these effects are ___15___ and laughter is followed by a period of muscle relaxation, ___16___ heart rate, ___17___ respiration, and decreased blood pressure. This period may last as long as 45 minutes. Some research has shown laughter causes a decrease in the levels of the stress hormones epinephrine, norepinephrine, and cortisol. This may explain the ___18___ between laughter and increased immune function, which leads to ___19___ health benefits. Scientific data supporting the extent and actual benefit of laughter is lacking, however, and some studies have ___20___ conflicting results.

Oral Activities

Activity One: Charades

Make a list of some unhealthy habits. Then work in pairs with one person miming the habits and the other one guessing what they are verbally.

Activity Two: Work in groups and discuss the following questions.

1. What are some tips to make people healthy, for example, how much sleep should a person get every night?
2. Discuss the relationship between physical health and mental health, giving examples when necessary. Offer some suggestions on how to deal with stress.

Activity Three: Dealing with Sub-health

According to a recent survey in 16 major Chinese cities with a population of over 1 million, surprisingly high proportions of urban Chinese have been suffering from problems related to sub-health. Some 75, 73, and 73 percent of Beijing, Shanghai and Guangzhou residents are in a subhealthy condition, in most cases among people with a high educational level.

Work in groups and discuss the reasons why people suffer from a subhealthy condition and propose some countermeasures to cope with this problem. Then present your results to the class.

Writing Practice

Note Writing: A Letter of Apology

Write a formal letter to your teacher, Mr. Johnson, apologizing to him for not attending his oral English class last Thursday because of your ankle injury.

_____ _____, 20_____

Dear Mr. Johnson,

Sincerely yours,

Composition Writing

College life can be very stressful. The competition for grades, the need to perform, the problems in relationships, the frustration in career choice, and many other aspects of the college environment cause stress. How can college students deal with their stress? Write a composition on the above issue and offer some solutions in about 120 words.

Unit 12 Memories

Warm-up Activities

1. Story-telling

    By telling stories, memory is passed down and kept alive. Answer the following questions, and based on the answers, tell a story about one of your own experiences.

   Questions:
   (1) What is the most unforgettable thing that happened to you or a friend?
   (2) Was it a happy or sad memory? Why?
   (3) What were the main events in the story?
   (4) How did things change later on?
   (5) What lesson(s) did you learn from the experience?

2. A saying goes that memories make the man. What's your understanding of it?

Text I

The 1896 Olympic Games in Athens

Pre-reading Questions

1. Have you ever read about the first modern Olympic Games? How much do you know about it?
2. Why were the first modern Olympic Games held in Athens?

Unit 12   Memories

1   Once the International Athletic Conference in Paris expressed its wish, the idea was welcomed with great enthusiasm by the press and public opinion in Greece. The press called upon the King to chair the organizing committee for the Games, thus providing an initial guarantee of their success. The government and the public authorities also were urged to assist in the endeavour, which was seen as a "task of national and public importance".

2   They believed that they were being given a chance to gain credibility in the eyes of other countries and to preserve their self-respect as a nation, which was undermined by the state of bankruptcy that the Greek government had declared in December 1893. As a ruined debtor to the great countries of Europe, the Greek government was unable to grant even token assistance to the production of the Games.

3   Further problems were caused by the fact that only fifteen or sixteen months were left to prepare for the Games, and by the limited sports facilities in Greece.

4   Vikelas and later Coubertin, had to travel to Athens from Pairs before these obstacles could be overcome. Coubertin was delighted by his stay in Greece. "*I am very enthusiastic about Athens,*" he wrote to Vikelas. "*It bustles with life. The Greeks have worked miracles. They are a great people, who have not disappointed my expectations from afar. I hoped that I would find Greece as I see it now, through my own eyes, and through yours.*"

5   Coubertin maintained these sincere feelings toward Greece throughout his life and they appear to have been the most important factor in his efforts to have the first Games held in Athens. He knew that if this endeavour, which had been so favourably commented on in the Greek and international press, were to fail, it would be much harder to keep alive the prospect of reviving the Olympic Games. All the experts agreed that failure to get the Olympic Games started would foil this unique opportunity to boost the world-wide athletic movement.

6   The revival of the Olympic idea opened new horizons in the search to renew values and ideals in many other areas, and Athens provided the best possible setting for their consolidation.

7 At the time, an increasing number of educators saw physical training as an essential component in the education of young people and as a medium by which their psychological and moral values could be shaped.

8 Vikelas firmly believed that the first international Olympic Games should at all costs be held in Greece, the country where the Olympic idea was born. Their organization should not be ostentatious, or this would allow the Greeks to set an example for others to follow. He feared that otherwise, the Olympic Games might never be revived.

9 Even before the Central Organizing Committee was formed and could request assistance, citizens from Greece and other countries, associations and guilds, hastened to announce in the newspapers that they would be subscribing to the Games or donating funds. These enthusiastic offers prompted the Committee, at its first meeting, to make an appeal for assistance to "Greeks the world over".

10 According to T. Philemon, it was decided not to accept donations from foreign nationals. Responses came from municipalities, consulates, monasteries, army units and the Greek communities in the Balkans, the Eastern Mediterranean, Odessa, Copenhagen, London, Ireland, Boston, Marseilles, Vienna, Cairo and elsewhere. Other ways were devised to support the committee's finances. On the suggestion of the Olympic Games Committee, the Greek government passed a law authorizing the issue of commemorative postage stamps and medallions with the Olympic Games theme. Combined with a generous donation of 585,000 drachmas from national benefactor George Averof, earmarked for restoring the marble in the Panathinaikon stadium, the total amount of money raised for the Games reached 1,500,000 drachmas, an astronomical sum by the standards of the time. These funds far exceeded the budget planned by Coubertin, who had calculated the cost of the Games at 150,000 drachmas. The money was used to restore the marble in the Panathinaikon stadium up to the level of the lower tier of seats. The work was later completed with another donation from Averof.

11 Among the facilities built were a shooting-range, a velodrome, lawn tennis courts, grand-stands for spectators at the rowing events, and boathouses. This was the first example of what might be called Olympic architecture, and the Central Organizing Committee of the first modern Olympic Games was successful in its efforts to meet the demands and specifications of the

international community.

12   In addition to the fund-raising difficulties, another obstacle to the Games' success emerged. This was the lack of interest by the British in the first Olympic Games, which was expressed in an article in the press. The British let it be known that if the Games were not organized according to standards in their country for running distances, regulations, etc., they would not consider the Games of the I Olympiad in Athens to be authentic.

13   Germany's participation was also in danger after the two largest sports associations in the country refused to attend the Games. The Germans based this decision on claims that they had been deliberately excluded from the First International Conference in Pairs and that the programme of the First Olympic Games did not give gymnastics its proper place.

14   Other crucial matters had to be carefully considered by the Central Committee to ensure the success of the Olympic Games. As this was the first athletic event of international scope, an estimate of the number of visitors was needed so that adequate accommodations could be provided. To be accepted by all countries, the programme of the Games had to include the right combination of sports; and the existing international regulations for the various sports had either to be adopted or revised, so that the participating countries would approve them. There was also the question of where to address the invitations, since the National Olympic Committees had yet to be established. Despite their lack of experience, the Central Committee found ingenious solutions to all these problems and the necessary sports facilities were built within a period of less than twelve months.

15   The Games of the I Olympiad opened with splendor at the newly built Panathinaikon Stadium on the 25th March, 1896. A Philharmonic orchestra, which included members from all the music clubs of Greece, performed the opening hymn. The lyrics of the Olympic Hymn were written by the Greek poet Costis Palamas and set to music by the Greek composer Spyros Samaras.

16   Already in the Games of the I Olympiad, the relationship between sports and music was well established. The Games opened and closed with the Olympic Anthem, which was eventually adopted by the Olympic Movement as the official Olympic Anthem. The Greek national anthem was also played at the ceremonies. This ritual continues to this day. It should be noted that when the Olympic Anthem was played at the stadium it awakened such a rush of emotion

and enthusiasm for Classical Greece that it was played a second time. Other pieces of music were played by the bands during the intermission periods. In the 1896 Games, the flag of each winner's country was raised and the band "saluted" it by playing a piece of music from the country; it was only with Louis's victory that the Greek national anthem was played.

17   Another tradition worthy of mention is the torch procession. In addition to its Classical connotations it also had a symbolic meaning: for the Greek people, fire is a symbol of re-birth and catharsis, but it also opens up new paths by illuminating the darkness, and draws people to gather around it for warmth.

18   Finally it should be pointed out that these ceremonies contributed greatly to the country's official diplomatic relations. The guests of honor—royalty and politicians from Britain, the Balkan countries and Egypt—were warmly received by the crowds in the stadium and at the other events.

19   The organization of the 1896 Olympic Games was a model for a subsequent Olympiads, not only in terms of its purely organizational aspects, but also in terms of its ceremonies and various cultural and social events. These Games also marked the beginning of the keen public interest which has been reflected in commemorative books, stamps and medals, the development of popular art related to the Games, and the attraction that this athletic institution has always held for artists and writers.

20   We should not forget that, when speaking of the re-birth of an institution, it is difficult to describe the process of its renaissance—including the problems to be overcome—concisely.

(1,452 words)

Words and Expressions

enthusiasm	/ɪn'θjuːzɪæzəm/	n.	a strong feeling of interest and enjoyment about something and an eagerness to be involved in it 热情，热忱
call upon			to request (正式)要求(某人做某事)
chair	/tʃeə/	vt.	to be the chairperson of a meeting or committee 当主席
bankruptcy	/'bæŋkrʌptsɪ/	n.	the state of being unable to pay your

Unit 12 Memories

			debts 无偿还能力, 破产, 倒闭
debtor	/ˈdetə/	n.	a person, group, or organization that owes money 债务人
grant	/grɑːnt/	vt.	to give someone something or allow them to have something that they have asked for 给予, 准予
token	/ˈtəʊkən/	adj.	done as a first sign that an agreement, promise, etc. will be kept and that more will be done later 象征性的
bustle	/ˈbʌsəl/	vi.	to move around quickly, looking very busy 忙忙碌碌, 忙乱
from afar			from a distance 从远处, 遥遥地
foil	/fɔɪl/	vt.	to prevent something bad that someone is planning to do 挫败
renew	/rɪˈnjuː/	vt.	to remove something that is old or broken and put a new one in its place 更新, 更换
consolidation	/kənˌsɒlɪˈdeɪʃən/	n.	the act of combining into an integral whole 联合
ostentatious	/ˌɒstənˈteɪʃəs/	adj.	looking very expensive and being designed to make people think that its owner must be very rich 铺张的, 豪华的
guild	/gɪld/	n.	an organization of people who do the same job or have the same interests 协会, 行会
hasten	/ˈheɪsən/	vi.	to do or say something quickly or without delay 急忙, 赶紧
prompt	/prɒmpt/	vt.	to make someone decide to do something 使下决心, 促使
donation	/dəʊˈneɪʃən/	n.	something, especially money, that you give to a person or an organization in order to help them 捐赠物(尤指捐款)
consulate	/ˈkɒnsjʊlɪt/	n.	the building in which a consul lives and works 领事馆
monastery	/ˈmɒnəstrɪ/	n.	a place where monks live 修道院, 寺院
devise	/dɪˈvaɪz/	vt.	to plan or invent a new way of doing something 想出, 设计出, 发明

commemorative	/kəˈmeməreɪtɪv/	adj.	intended to make people remember 纪念的
drachma	/ˈdrækmə/	n.	the standard unit of money used in Greece before the euro 德拉克马（现代希腊原货币单位）
astronomical	/ˌæstrəˈnɒmɪkəl/	adj.	extremely high 极高的
tier	/tɪə/	n.	one of several rows or layers of something, especially seats, that rise one behind another（尤指座位的）一排，一列
shooting-range		n.	a place where people shoot guns at objects to win prizes 射击场
velodrome	/ˈveləUr dr əʊm/	n.	a circular track used for bicycle racing（有圆形赛道的）自行车赛车场
spectator	/spekˈteɪtə/	n.	someone who is watching an event or game 观众，观看者
boathouse	/ˈbəʊˌhaʊs/	n.	a building beside a lake or river where boats are kept 停船场所，停船棚屋
specification	/ˌspesɪfɪˈkeɪʃən/	n.	a requirement which is clearly stated 明细规范
fund-raising	/ˈfʌndˌreɪzɪŋ/	n.	the activity of collecting money to support a charity or political campaign or organization 资金筹集（工作）
address	/əˈdres/	vt.	to put an address on an envelope, package, etc. 在（信封、包裹等）上写姓名地址
ingenious	/ɪnˈdʒiːnɪəs/	adj.	(of a thing) cleverly made or planned and involving new ideas and methods 巧妙的
splendor	/ˈsplendə/	n.	impressive beauty, especially of a large building or large place 壮观，华丽
Philharmonic	/ˌfɪləːˈmɒnɪk/	adj.	used in the names of orchestras 爱乐的（用于管弦乐队的名称中）
hymn	/hɪm/	n.	a song of praise (to God or to a saint or to a nation) 赞歌，圣歌，凯歌
lyric	/ˈlɪrɪk/	n.	the words of a song 歌词
national anthem			the official song of a nation that is sung or played on public occasions 国歌
ritual	/ˈrɪtʃʊəl/	n.	a ceremony that is always performed in

Unit 12 Memories

			the same way, in order to mark an important religious or social occasion 仪式，典礼
intermission	/ˌɪntəˈmɪʃən/	n.	a short period of time between the parts of a play, concert, etc. 幕间休息
procession	/prəˈseʃən/	n.	a line of people or vehicles moving slowly as part of a ceremony（人或车辆的）行列，游行队伍
connotation	/ˌkɒnəˈteɪʃən/	n.	a quality or an idea that a word makes you think of, which is more than its basic meaning 隐含意义，内涵意义，联想含义
catharsis	/kəˈθɑːsɪs/	n.	the act or process of removing strong or violent emotions by expressing them through writing, talking, acting, etc. 宣泄，精神发泄
illuminate	/ɪˈluːmɪneɪt/	vt.	to make a light shine on something, or to fill a place with light 照亮，照射
diplomatic relation			relationships between countries 外交关系
guest of honour			the most important guest 贵宾
royalty	/ˈrɔɪəlti/	n.	members of a royal family 王室（皇族）成员
Olympiad	/əˈlɪmpiæd/	n.	a particular occasion of the modern Olympic Games（现代）奥林匹克运动会
renaissance	/rɪˈneɪsəns/	n.	a new interest in something, especially a particular form of art, music, etc., that has not been popular for a long period 复兴

Notes:

Vikelas was the first president of the International Olympic Committee.
the Balkans is a large area in southeast Europe which includes Greece, Romania, Bulgaria, Albania and Yugoslavia. It is an area in which there have been many wars and many changes in the borders of the countries.
the Mediterranean is the area of southern Europe that surrounds the Mediterranean Sea.
Odessa is a city in the U.S. state of Texas.

Copenhagen   is the capital and largest city of Denmark.
Boston   is the capital and largest city of Massachusetts.
Marseilles   is the second-largest city of France.
Vienna   is the capital of Austria.
Cairo   is the capital and largest city of Egypt.
Panathenaikon Statdium   is in Athens. It is the only major stadium in the world built fully of white marble.
Olympic Anthem   also known as the Olympic Hymn, is a musical piece. The anthem was performed for the first time for the opening ceremony at the 1896 Athens Olympic Games.

Reading Comprehension

I. Summarize the following situations according to the text.

1. The difficulties in the first modern Olympiad

2. The traditions established by the first modern Olympiad

II. Answer the following questions.

1. How did the Greeks respond to the idea of holding the first modern Olympic?

2. Why did Coubertin and Vikelas choose Greece as the host nation for the first modern Olympic Games? Explain the reasons respectively.

3. How was the fund for the first modern Olympic Games raised?

4. What music was played in the I Olympiad at ceremonies and intermission periods?

5. What is the connotation of the Olympic torch procession?

Unit 12 Memories

III. **Judge, according to the text, whether the following statements are true or false. For false statements, write the facts in parentheses.**
   1. There was then only one year for the preparation of the first modern Olympic Games.
      (   )
   2. Vikelas deeply believed that the first international Olympic Games should at all costs be held in Greece.
      (   )
   3. After the establishment of the Central Organizing Committee, many announced in the newspaper that they would donate for the games.
      (   )
   4. It was decided not to accept donations from foreign nationals for the first modern Olympic Games.
      (   )
   5. The first modern Olympic Games were the first athletic event of international scope.
      (   )

IV. **Paraphrase the following sentences within the context.**
   1. (Para. 2) They believed that they were being given a chance to gain credibility in the eyes of other countries and to preserve their self-respect as a nation, which was undermined by the state of bankruptcy that the Greek government had declared in December 1893.
      _____
      _____

   2. (Para. 5) All the experts agreed that failure to get the Olympic Games started would foil this unique opportunity to boost the world-wide athletic movement.
      _____
      _____

   3. (Para. 9) These enthusiastic offers prompted the Committee, at its first meeting, to make an appeal for assistance to "Greeks the world over".
      _____
      _____

4. **(Para. 10)** On the suggestion of the Olympic Games Committee, the Greek government passed a law authorizing the issue of commemorative postage stamps and medallions with the Olympic Games theme.

_____

_____

Vocabulary Exercises

I. **Fill in each blank with one of the following words from each group and note the difference in meaning among them. Change the form when necessary.**

1. **PRESERVE   CONSERVE   RESERVE**

   a. These yellow seats are _____ for the elderly and women with babies.

   b. We are cutting down on our central heating to _____ electricity.

   c. No one knows for sure how people first learned to _____ food.

   d. The other members accepted my advice without _____.

   e. We must _____ our existing woodlands for future generations.

   f. The president has promised that the government is committed to the _____ of the country's national interests.

2. **ASSESSMENT   ESTIMATE   EVALUATION**

   a. It was difficult to _____ how many trees had been destroyed in the earthquake.

   b. The value of his business was _____ at £1.25 million.

   c. _____ of the new system cannot take place until all the data has been collected.

   d. You should be able to _____ the quality of your own work.

   e. The expert believes that it is important to _____ the impact of advertising on children.

   f. The mechanic gave me a rough _____ of two or three hundred dollars for the repairs to my car.

Unit 12   Memories

II. Fill in the blank in each sentence with a word or phrase taken from the box. Change the form where necessary.

endeavour	commemorative	boost	rush of
foil	ostentatious	earmark	set an example
open up	ingenious		

1. The umbrella was _____ devised to fold up into your pocket.
2. Despite our best _____, we couldn't get the car started in such a cold day.
3. The local government has announced plans to _____ access to higher education.
4. A statue has been erected to _____ the 300th anniversary of the poet's birthday.
5. The discovery of Roman ruins has _____ tourism in this area.
6. Half of this year's budget is already _____ for hospital improvements.
7. She felt a cold _____ air as she opened her window.
8. The man took out his gold watch and laid it _____ on the table in front of him.
9. Education experts suggest that parents should _____ for their children.
10. The prisoners' attempt to escape was _____ at the last minute.

III. Choose a word or phrase that best completes each of the following sentences.

1. The investigation showed that a cigarette stub _____ yesterday's fire in the department store.
    A. ignited   B. immersed   C. illuminated   D. ignored
2. I'm afraid the tour of Disneyland will _____ a lot of money as well as time.
    A. call in   B. call out   C. call for   D. call upon
3. The drowning child was saved by Nick's _____ action.
    A. acute   B. alert   C. profound   D. prompt
4. The company _____ the customer's wish and sent the delivery overnight.
    A. furnished   B. accommodated   C. afforded   D. provided

5. _____ modern science and technology, they tended to use the myths as a way of understanding nature and human behavior.
   A. Lack   B. Lacked   C. Lacking   D. Being lacked

Translation Exercises

Translate each of the following sentences into English, using the words or phrase given in the bracket.

1. 国际红十字总会紧急呼吁社会各界捐款捐物，积极参与地震灾害的救助工作。(call upon)

2. 牛奶供应商联合向公众郑重承诺，要不惜一切代价保证乳品安全，确保消费者的身体健康。(at all costs)

3. 由于学前教育的过度市场化，有些幼儿园的收费远远超过大学，给收入偏低的家庭带来了巨大的经济负担。(exceed)

4. 第一届现代奥运会沿袭了古代奥运会的传统，将妇女排除在外，不设女子比赛项目。(exclude from)

5. 在董事会上，大家都发言赞成我的年度销售方案，这使我感到无比欣慰和自豪。(in favor of)

6. 得知儿子在战争中牺牲，他禁不住泪如泉涌，一时无法接受这突如其来的噩耗。(a rush of)

7. 《哈利·波特》系列魔幻小说已被译成64种语言，受到世界各地少年读者的欢迎，全球总销量达3.25亿册。(receive)

Unit 12 Memories

Text II

I Remember...

> **Pre-reading Questions**
>
> 1. Is there a song that can bring back a strong memory of your childhood? What would be your most treasured memory of your childhood?
> 2. What TV program is your favorite? What influence has it exerted on you?

1   We got our TV set in 1959, when I was 5. So I can barely remember life without television. I have spent 20,000 hours of my life in front of the set. Not all of my contemporaries watched so much, but many did, and what's more, we watched the same programs, heard the same commercials, were exposed to the same end-of-show lessons. So there is, among this generation of television children, a shared history, a tremendous fund of common experience. These massive doses of TV have not affected all of us in an identical way, and it would be risky to draw broad conclusions. But if a sociologist were —rashly—to try to uncover some single most important influence on this generation, which has produced Patty Hearst and Alice Cooper and the Jesus movement and the peace movement; if he were searching for the roots of 1960's psychedelia and 1970's apathy, he would do well to look first at television.

2   My own motives are less ambitious. I know, simply, that a rerun of *I Love Lucy* or *Father Knows Best*, the theme music from *Dr. Kildare* or the sad, whistling refrain from *Lassie* can make me stand, frozen, before the set. It is as if I, and not Timmy Martin, had been stuck in an abandoned mine shaft during a thunderstorm, as if I, and not Lucy Ricardo, had dropped a diamond ring somewhere in the batter of a seven-layer cake. I didn't so much watch those shows when I was little; I let them wash over me. Now I study them like a psychiatrist on his own couch, looking hungrily for some clue inside the TV set to explain the person I have become.

3   I was not a dull or energyless child, or neglected by my parents. Our house was full of books and paints, and sometimes I did choose to draw or ride my

bike. But the picture of my childhood that comes to mind is one of a dimly lit room in a small New Hampshire town and a girl listening, leaden-eyed, to some talk-show rendition of "I Left My Heart in San Francisco". It is a picture of myself at age 8, wise to the ways of "Vegas," the timing of standup comics, the marriages of Zsa Zsa Gabor, the advertising slogans of Bufferin and Fab.

4   And what did all this television watching teach me? Well, I rarely swallowed the little pellets of end-of-show morals presented in the television shows I watched (that crime does not pay, that one must always obey one's parents). But I observed something of the way the world works: that life is easier if one fits in with the established conventions; that everything is easier if one has a pretty face.

5   And in the process of acquiring those melancholy truths I picked up an embarrassingly large fund of knowledge that is totally unusable (except, perhaps, ironically, on some television game show). I can hum Perry Mason's theme song or give the name of the actress who played Donna Reed's best friend. I would happily trade that knowledge for the facility with piano or ballet I might have had if I'd spent those television hours practicing music and dance instead. But something else I gained from television should be less lightly dismissed. I guess it is a sense of knowing America, not simply its vulgarities but its strengths as well: the rubber face of Lucille Ball, the lovableness of Americans on *Candid Camera*, an athlete's slow-motion grace in an instant replay on *Monday Night Football*.

6   So many hours of television I watched—hundreds of bank robberies, touch-and-go operations and barroom fights, millions of dollars' worth of refrigerators awarded to thousands of housewives who kissed dozens of game-show moderators—and yet the list of individual programs I remember is very short. One is the Beatles' appearance, the winter I was 10, on *The Ed Sullivan Show*. I remember the on-camera shooting of Lee Oswald, and the face of Jacqueline Kennedy at her husband's funeral. A few particularly marvelous episodes of the old *Dick Van Dyke Show* stand out: Laura Petrie getting her toe stuck in the bathroom faucet; Rob imaging that he's going bald. One or two *I*

Love Lucy, Andy Griffith shows, a Miss America contestant who sang a number from "The sound of music"—dressed like a nun—and then whipped off her habit to reveal a spangled bathing suit. I remember a special five-part *Dr. Kildare* segment in which a team of doctors had to choose five patients for a lifesaving kidney machine out of eight candidates. I remember getting up at midnight to watch Neil Armstrong land on the moon—expecting to be awed, but falling asleep instead.

My strongest memories are of one series and one character. Not the best, but the one that formed me more than any other, that haunts me still, and left its mark on a good-sized part of a generation: *Leave It to Beaver*, I watched that show every day after school and studied it, like homework, because the Cleaver family was so steady and normal—and my own was not—and because the boys had so many friends, played basketball, drank sodas, fit in. Watching that series and other family situation comedies was almost like taking a course in how to be an American.

I loved my father, but I longed secretly for a "Dad" like Ward Cleaver, who puttered in a work shed, building bookcases and oiling hinges, one who spent his Saturday afternoons playing golf or mowing the lawn or dipping his finger into cake batter whipped up by a mother in a frilly apron who spent her time going to PTA meetings and playing bridge with "the girls". Wally Cleaver, the older brother, was one of those boys destined to be captain of every team he plays on. But Beaver had his problems—often he was uncoordinated, gullible, less than perfectly honest, tricked by his older brother's friends, made fun of. He lost library books and haircut money. Once he sent away for a "free" accordion and suddenly found himself wildly in debt. Of course he got caught—he always did. I remember him so clearly, as familiar to me as a brother.

Occasionally I go to college campuses. Some student in the audience always mentions Beaver Cleaver, and when the name is spoken, a satisfied murmur can be heard in the crowd. Somebody—a stranger, in his 20s now—wrote to say he watches Beaver reruns every morning. He just wanted to share memories of the show with me and recall favorite episodes. We were not readers, after all, this stranger and I. We have no great literary tradition behind us. Our heritage is television. Wally and Beaver Cleaver were our Tom Sawyer and Huck Finn.

There's something terribly sad about this need to reminisce, and the lack of real stories, true experiences, to reminisce about. Partly it is that we grew up in the '60s, when life was soft, and partly that we grew up with television, which made life softer. We had Vietnam, of course, and civil-rights battles, and a brief threat of nuclear attack that led neighbors, down the block, to talk of building a fallout shelter. But I remember the large events, like the Kennedy and King assassinations, the space launches and the war, as I experienced them through television. I watched it all from a goose-down-filled easy chair with a plate of oatmeal cookies on my lap—on television.

11 We grew up to be observers, not participants, to respond to action, not initiate it. And I think finally, it was this lack of real hardship that was our greatest hardship and that led so many among this television generation to seek out some kind of artificial pain. Some of us, for a time at least, gave up matching skirt-and-sweater sets for saffron-colored Hare Krishna robes; some gave up parents and clean-cut fiancés for the romance of poverty and the excitement of crime. Rebellion like that is not so much inspired by television violence as it is brought about by television banality: it is a response not to *The Man from U.N.C.L.E.* but to *Father Knows Best*. One hears it said that hatred of an idea is closer to love than to indifference. Large and angry rejections of the bourgeois, the conventional—the Beaver Cleaver life—aren't so surprising, coming from a generation that grew up admiring those things so much.

12 Television smartened us up, expanded our minds, and then proceeded to fill them with the only kinds of knowledge it had to offer: names of Las Vegas nightclubs, brands of detergent, players of bit parts. And knowledge—accurate or not—about life: marriage as we learned about it from Ozzie and Harriet, justice as practiced by Matt Dillon, politics as revealed to us on the 6 o'clock news.

13 Anguished, frustrated and enraged by a decade of war in Vietnam as we saw it on the news, we became part of the news ourselves—with peace marches, rallies in the streets. But only briefly; we were easily discouraged, quick to abandon hope for change and to lose interest. That, also, comes from a television-watching childhood, I think: a short attention span, and a limpness, an inertia, acquired from too many hours spent in the easy chair, never getting up except to change the channels.

(1,589 words)

Unit 12 Memories

Reading Comprehension

I. **Answer the following questions with the information you read from the passage.**
1. Why would a sociologist turn to television if he/she were to try to find out some influence on the generation of 60s and 70s?
2. What did the author acquire from all the television watching?
3. How did the characters such as "Ward Cleaver", "Wally Cleaver", etc. influence the author? Why?
4. In the author's view, what caused some of his/her generation to be TV addicts?
5. List all the TV programs or characters mentioned in the passage and talk with your partners about how they influenced the author.

II. **Topics for discussion and reflection.**
1. Memories are very precious to people's lives. They give us the opportunity to prove to ourselves that we exist, and if we lose them, we have an unrelenting fear of uncertainty. Talk with your partners about the significance of memory in people life.
2. In what aspects does TV influence our life, such as moral behaviors, cultural values, etc.?

Exercises for Integrated Skills

I. **Dictation**

   Listen to the following passage. Altogether the passage will be read to you four times. During the first reading, which will be read at normal speed, listen and try to understand the meaning. For the second and third readings, the passage will be read sentence by sentence, or phrase by phrase, with intervals of 15 to 20 seconds. The last reading will be done at normal speed again and during this time you should check your work. You will then be given 2 minutes to check through your work once more.

II. Cloze

Fill in each blank in the passage below with a word or phrase taken from the box in its appropriate form.

comfort	fragile	loose	silent	blow
huddle	destruct	gaze	crash	lifetime
fleet	relive	burst	newborn	intent
joy	leave	immerse	blur	controllable

Can it really be sixty-two years ago that I first saw you? It is truly a ___1___, I know. But as I ___2___ into your eyes now, it seems like only yesterday that I first saw you, in that small café in Hanover Square.

From the moment I saw you smile, as you opened the door for that young mother and her ___3___ baby. I knew, I knew that I wanted to share the rest of my life with you.

I still think of how foolish I must have looked, as I gazed at you, that first time. I remember watching you ___4___, as you took off your hat and ___5___ shook your short dark hair with your fingers. I felt myself becoming ___6___ in your every detail, as you placed your hat on the table and cupped your hands around the hot cup of tea, gently ___7___ the steam away with your pouted lips.

From that moment, everything seemed to make perfect sense to me. The people in the café and the busy street outside all disappeared into a hazy ___8___. All I could see was you.

All through my life I ___9___ that every first day. Many, many times I have sat and thought about the first day, and how for a few ___10___ moments I am there, feeling again what is like to know true love for the very first time. It pleases me that I can still have those feelings now after all those years, and I know I will always have them to ___11___ me.

Not even as I shook and trembled ___12___ in the trenches, did I forget your face. I would sit ___13___ into the wet mud, terrified, as the hails of bullets and mortars ___14___ down around me. I would clutch my rifle tightly to my heart, and think again of that very first day we met. I would cry out in fear, as the noise of war beat down around me. But, as I thought of you and saw you smiling back at me, everything around me would become ___15___, and I would be with you again for a few precious moments, far from the death and ___16___. It would not be until I opened my eyes once again, that I would see and hear the carnage of the war around me.

I cannot tell you how strong my love for you was back then, when I returned to you on ___17___ in September, feeling battered, bruised and ___18___. We held each other so tight that I thought we would ___19___. I asked you to marry me the very same day and I whooped with ___20___ when you looked deep into my eyes and said "yes" to being my bride.

Oral Activities

Activity One: An Unforgettable Memory

Talk about an unforgettable memory in your life, including the moment of your first attempt at something or the one that changed your life—an unforgettable studying experience, either painful or delightful.

Activity Two: Work in groups and discuss the following questions.

1. How can one's childhood memories influence his/her life when he/she grows up? For example, if a child was often beaten by his/her parents, he tends to be violent as a grown-up.
2. What are some of the bitter and glorious memories of sports in China? What are the decisive moments in China's sporting development?

Writing Practice

Letter Writing: A Letter of Sympathy

Your friend was injured in a car accident and has been sent to a hospital. Write a letter to him/her to show your sympathy.

15 June, 20____

Dear,

Yours,

Composition Writing

"Every man's memory is his private literature." What is the most unforgettable memory in your life? Based on the outcome of oral activities, write a composition about your memory and its influence on you in about 120 words.

References

Baker, Peter. (2001) Making the Best of a Good Job. *English Learning*. Beijing: Foreign Language Teaching and Research Press.

Friedan, Betty. (2006) The Feminine Mystique. *The New York Times*. February 5.

Hyndman, Donald. (2006) We Are the Problem from The Future Where Do We Go from Here? *Disasters*. Courrier Corporational Kendallville.

Josepha, Sherman. (2003) Prometheus Steals Fire—A Myth of Ancient Greeks. *Mythology for Storyteller-themes and Tales from around the World*. New York: Armonk.

Krebs, Hans-Dieter. (2001) Sport and Music. *Olympic Review*. February.

Maynard, Joyce. (1987) *I Remember... 75 Readings: A Freshman Anthology*. McGraw-Hill, Inc.

Merritt, Stephamie. (1990) *Music and Healing. Mind, Music and Imagery*. First Published by Plume, an imprint of Penguin Books. U.S.A. Inc.

Schnur, Steven. (2004) A Father's Walk to School. *The Christian Science Monitor*. October 20.

Terasawa, Yoshio. (1974) Japanese Style in Decision-Making. *The New York Times*. Sunday May 12.

Wickersham, John M. (2000) Modern Mythology. *Myths and Legends of the World*. Volume 3. New York: An Imprint of the Gale Group.

Widdowson, H.G. (1978) Kinship and the Family. *English in Social Studies*. Oxford: Oxford University Press.

何兆熊.(2005)《综合教程》(新世纪高等院校英语专业本科生系列教材).上海:上海外语教育出版社.

田慧.(2008)《现代英汉汉英体育大词典》.北京:人民体育出版社.

田慧,朱珠.(2007)《体育英语报刊选读》.北京:北京大学出版社.

田慧,李晶.(2007)《走近奥运》.北京:北京体育大学出版社.

http://www.guardian.co.uk/education/2006/jul/25/highereducation.mbas

http://www.gzedu.com.cn/vip/article/2008-7-3/9965-1.htm

http://www.jbpub.com/samples/0763741450/Edlin_Health%20and%20Wellness_9e_Ch_01.pdf

http://www.kingkong.demon.co.uk/gsr/silkstox.htm

http://www.la84foundation.org/OlympicInformationCenter/OlympicReview/2001/OREXXVII38/OREXXVII38h.pdf

http://www.olympic.org/upload/news/olympic_review/review_2005628172259_UK.pdf

http://www.rd.com/a-tornado-traps-children-in-a-crumbled-school/article49096.html

http://www.rd.com/living-healthy/wife-donates-a-kidney-to-husband/article28506.html